From Kitchen  ᴛᴏ *Market*

Selling Your Gourmet Food Specialty

3rd Edition

STEPHEN F. HALL

DEARBORN™
TRADE

A **Kaplan Professional** Company

This publication is designed to provide accurate and authoritative information in regard to the subject matter covered. It is sold with the understanding that the publisher is not engaged in rendering legal, accounting, or other professional service. If legal advice or other expert assistance is required, the services of a competent professional person should be sought.

Acquisitions Editor: Mary B. Good
Senior Managing Editor: Jack Kiburz
Interior Design: Eliot House Productions
Cover Design: Studio Montage

Published by Dearborn Trade, a Kaplan Professional Company

Printed in the United States of America

00 01 02 10 9 8 7 6 5 4 3 2 1

Library of Congress Cataloging-in-Publication Data

Hall, Stephen F.
    From kitchen to market : selling your gourmet food specialty /
Stephen F. Hall.— 3rd ed.
      p.   cm.
    Includes bibliographical references and index.
    ISBN 0-8225-1744-2
    1. Food industry and trade—United States. 2. Food service—United
States. I. Title.
    HD9004 .H25 2000
    664'.0068'8—dc21
                                                          00-009762

Contents

Acknowledgments to the Third Edition

I am grateful for Gourmet America President Ron Johnson's level headed and healthy enthusiasm about the specialty food trade. His observations have balanced well with some of the highly entrepreneurial processes we see among the new-to-market food processors. I am indebted also to the editors of *New Product News* for their insights into specialty food trends, and to my older son, Tully, for his assistance in surfing the Internet to find and confirm extensive appendix information (and, to "cover the bases," hello to my younger son, Colin).

Acknowledgments to the Second Edition

In addition to the good souls listed below, I acknowledge gladly the advice and valuable counsel I received from Karen Cantor, the driving spirit and publisher of *Food Entrepreneur* magazine, and the altogether exhaustive reference-building by my wife, Patricia Teagle.

Acknowledgments to the First Edition

First and foremost, I am grateful to my wife, Patricia Teagle, for her unending good humor and editorial counsel. Many thanks, also, to my colleagues in the specialty food business, particularly Ron Johnson, of Gourmet America, Inc., who provided important viewpoints in defining how specialty food marketing works; Elliot Johnson, of Mark T. Wendell Co., for the precision with which he assesses industry trends; Liz and Nick Thomas, of Chalif, Inc., who provided comprehensive and altogether helpful reviews of the first draft of this guide; Barry Raskin, a specialty food broker largely responsible for guiding me during my early education in this field; Ernie Fisher, an international food consultant who brought a "real world" perspective to examining this industry; and to Lee Robinson, who, as President of The Ruffled Truffle, provided me with the opportunity to learn about the gift segment of the specialty food business.

I am grateful, further, to Page Pratt, co-founder of Food Marketing International, with whom I shared many a rewarding marketing moment, and to my editor, Jean Kerr, whose unflappable disposition eased the burden of perfecting this book.

Finally, I would like to acknowledge my late colleague, classmate and best friend, Rolff Johansen, for bringing civility and wit to our hectic earlier years in specialty food marketing.

How to Use This Guide

From Kitchen to Market helps you learn about marketing food, a process that generally entails everything from product concept to after-sales service. This edition addresses important, and developing, aspects of specialty food marketing not addressed in previous editions, and provides up-to-date information in the Appendices.

In addition to packaging, labeling, pricing, storage, and shipping, the guide tells you how to advertise, promote, and sell your product. Flowcharts describe how to process the orders you generate. Major sections include "Guidelines for Success" that you may use as you prepare to take your product to market. New sections deal with how to exploit overseas opportunities, the impact of technology (the Internet), and how to grow your enterprise. In other words: how to professionalize your business.

"Cases in Point" are used throughout the book to highlight so-called real world experiences. In this edition, those Cases in Point identify the successes, and failures, of many winners of "Outstanding Product Awards," the purpose being to show you that it takes more than an award to ensure your success.

From Kitchen to Market is designed for small, cottage industries new to the food business, but it will also be of significant value to large food processors and overseas food companies interested in learning how the U.S. specialty food trade functions.

Specialty food marketing is addressed in a straightforward, logical manner. It begins with introductory comments, followed by a general discussion of the industry. It proceeds to discuss the issues relevant to getting your product ready to market, and to taking your product to market. The appendices offer information about additional sources of assistance along with useful data regarding trade shows, trade journals, professional associations, etc.

Other helpful resources from Dearborn include *The Business Planning Guide: Creating a Plan for Success in Your Own Business*. *The Business Planning Guide* leads business owners through the most important step in founding a new business: putting together a complete and effective business plan and financing proposal.

Also, *Steps to Small Business Start-Up: Everything You Need to Know to Turn Your Idea Into a Successful Business* for anyone who wants hands-on, practical information about starting and running a business.

You will probably not need this guide if your name is Paul Newman. Deep pockets can make the difference between success or failure for a high quality product. If, like the rest of us, you have neither the funding level to support a major marketing effort, nor the clout to see it through, then this guide is for you.

Before you begin you need to answer the question: Do you want your food operation to be a full-time occupation or a sideline business?

One of the following scenarios may describe your circumstances, and could help you respond to the important issue of just how involved you would like to become in the business. All four of these scenarios have been played out, with varying degrees of success, in the gourmet food industry.

Scenario One

You have just returned from another successful holiday church bazaar where you sold out your homemade supply of apple-cranberry chutney. Your chutney is based on a family recipe handed down for generations. Your friends and neighbors urge you to sell your chutney to

Bloomingdale's, where they think it will be a great hit. You think it's a wonderful idea, but you haven't the foggiest idea of where to begin.

In this scenario, the entrepreneur has to decide, after significant investigation, whether or not to continue in the "sideline" mode, or to take the risk of turning the operation into a full-time business.

On the one hand, the owner has a product that has been tested, in a fashion, with positive reactions from customers, friends, and neighbors. There is reason to believe that success, at least initially, might be achieved with a reasonable expectation of profit. On the other hand, what is the required level of funding available for the venture? If the owner has an outside source of income, then the venture may be undertaken. Otherwise, the possibilities for negative cash flow (more money going out than coming in) are quite probable.

Scenario Two

Your gourmet food store is doing a lot of business. You are especially pleased with the success of your prepared foods section, one item of which is your home-baked, seasoned, bread sticks. You note that there seems to be a growing interest in this product from a broad segment of your customer base. You wonder if it would be possible to sell the bread sticks to a wider audience in other markets in your region. Where to begin?

If the second scenario fits, then revenues from the existing retail operation could support your food marketing venture. This makes market entry more attractive because many initial costs of operation could be absorbed by the retail store sales of other products. Nevertheless, you will have to devote substantial time to developing markets for the bread sticks, which will take away from time spent in the store. If this can be accommodated, then a full-time sales and marketing operation can be adopted.

Scenario Three

You have recently taken over a small, local, chocolate manufacturer. Until now, revenues have come from bulk sales to walk-in and mail-order customers. You think there are substantial opportunities for developing a retail packaged version, and you want to begin distributing it to stores all over the country. How do you proceed?

Scenario three offers some of the same challenges as scenario two. Both require substantial time at the existing business. Scenario three, however, offers a chance to expand an existing base of sales to customers located outside of the local area. It also provides an existing source of revenue (from retail-packaged sales) on which to base some of the expansion costs. It would appear, then, that turning the chocolate operation into a full-time sales and marketing operation might be an appropriate alternative.

Scenario Four

Your family and friends love your honey and pecan mustard. You have been very successful in selling at the local Women's Exchange, and at area school holiday fairs. You also ran an ad in a slick "upscale" magazine that cost you a fortune, but produced results in mail-order sales sufficient to cover the cost. Your life is too busy to contemplate going into the gourmet food business full time. What do you need to know about this business in order to make a little money on the side?

The challenge in scenario four is to make your hobby into a sideline business. You can take your talent, your recipes, your promotional genius, and your money, and have your product produced, packaged, warehoused, and marketed by another company. You will definitely need the supporting funds and the knowledge of how gourmet food marketing works.

Your situation may differ from these scenarios, but the opportunity to turn your food ideas into an endeavor for financial independence prevails. The gourmet food business is one way of obtaining a significant shot at achieving success and acquiring wealth.

Now that you are armed with a sense of which option best applies to your situation, read on to learn how to take the next step in the exciting and challenging world of gourmet food marketing.

A Note about the Illustrations

Product appearance is one of the most important components of success in the specialty food industry. In order to give you a flavor of this, and to stimulate your imagination, I have included a representative sampling of graphics used in a variety of specialty food labels, packages, and company logos. These have been placed throughout the book, in no particular order.

The illustrations selected were among those requested from more than 100 companies whose products have been exhibited in various National Association for the Specialty Food Trade Shows over the past ten years.

A number of these are designed for application in color, but, because of cost constraints, they have been reproduced here in black and white. Many of them are effective attention-getters with the use of only two colors. The objective is to emphasize the importance of graphics, regardless of color, in label, package, and logo design.

The examples in this book are those deemed typical, both good and, perhaps, not so good, for this industry. You be the judge. And, please note that use of them does not constitute an endorsement.

Introduction

The specialty foods industry is generating retail revenues of almost $39 billion a year and is averaging annual growth of around 7 percent. To some, this means great opportunity. To others, it represents a formidable challenge.

Your ability to grab a slice of this pie, and make your mark, establish your independence, achieve success, and acquire wealth, will depend on how effectively you prepare—and prepare you must!

How to prepare for the opportunities and challenges of taking your food products to the appropriate store shelves is the subject of this guide. You need not know the basics of small business operations just yet. For now, success will depend on your personal and business vision, drive, talent, and the amount of capital you can raise.

Let's put the latter into perspective: the average cost of getting national grocery store shelf exposure for a new product by a branded manufacturer is $5.1 million.[*]

---

[*] This figure comes from a 1991 study by a Joint Industry Task Force consisting of the Grocery Manufacturers of America, Food Marketing Institute, National American Wholesale Grocers Association, National Association of Chain Drug Stores, National Food Brokers Association, and National Grocer Association.

Still reading? Take heart, there is a proven alternative. It is the specialty food industry that has become the proven vehicle for entry-level food distribution in the United States. Different market segments and new products can be tested in the specialty food industry without the initial investment required of the major food producers. The secret has to do with superior execution of often ordinary ideas.

Having said that, you must pay heed to a recently developed phenomena called "slotting fees" (see Chapter 3 for more details). The advent of the slotting fee has drastically altered the complexion of specialty food marketing in this country. The slotting fee is, for all intents and purposes, what used to be called "payola." It is up-front money paid to the chain or distributor in order to have your product carried. It severely limits consumer choice and producer competition. Unless your marketing plan is just plain brilliantly and flawlessly executed, it means that new and alternative distribution must be explored. It will have an impact on the role of the Internet.

How Much Will It Cost You?

Depending on your approach, you can expect to incur minimum start-up costs of approximately $35,000 to $100,000 **or more** for each year for the first three to five years. This includes production, packaging, labeling, advertising, and promotion of one product. It does NOT include the cost of success. Many firms that won Outstanding Product Awards were ill prepared for the next move. Not all of them succeeded in profiting from their good fortune. The estimated cost also is based on the assumption that you will be doing a lot of the leg work. (Example: You do all of the administrative, invoicing, clerical paperwork, and you make most of the sales calls.)

Our purpose is to explore the inner workings of *niche* marketing. Niche marketing entails finding the best combination of product packaging, pricing, positioning, and promotion that will encourage the consumer to purchase a product not otherwise offered by the major suppliers. Imagination is a key ingredient, but adequate funding is essential.

> "You'll need more than a dream to carry you across the starting line," says Liz Thomas, Former Exec. VP, Chalif, Inc.

In addition to the above, a successful undertaking requires you to center your activities on your competitive strengths, control your costs, know your competition, and learn how to professionally manage the entire process effectively. As with most new food entrepreneurs, you will have to learn to deal with finding resources, motivating employees, developing a compelling vision, and even handling family issues.

We are not addressing here what you can do with a several million dollar budget. Rather, this guide deals with the essence of entrepreneurship. There is a lot of "ready, fire, aim" in the gourmet food marketing process that can lead to some success and frequent failure. This guide helps you accomplish most of the "aiming" during the "ready" phase.

Specialty food marketing requires creative responses. As soon as you adopt a successful marketing strategy, you may learn of another entrepreneur who is just as successful, but who has implemented an entirely different marketing scheme!

✧   ✧   ✧

The 1970s: "The Specialty Food business is an odd little segment of the industry that is better left to people who understand it fully, who deeply care about it, and who are willing to have a less predictable bottom line than most corporations are willing to tolerate," says Ted Koryn, specialty food marketing professional, as quoted in *Fortune* magazine, October 1978.

The 2000s: "Specialty food has come a long way from its easy-to-understand description of . . . exotic, ethnic, imported, unusual, and sold in a department or gourmet store. Today, it is much more complex. Thousands of new domestically produced specialty items . . . fit in established and high-volume product categories [are] sold in all types of retail formats."

—John Roberts, President, National Association for the Specialty Food Trade (NASFT)

CHAPTER ONE

Understanding the Food Industry

This chapter defines industry terms, examines the primary sales territories and segments of the market, and describes transition products—those that make the transition from gourmet to grocery (the "big time")—along with a discussion of a typical gourmet retail store operation.

Defining the Territory

The food industry, in general, and the specialty food industry, in particular, has yet to sanction specific guidelines for the use of many industry terms. As a result, the process of tracking and understanding the myriad elements of specialty food sales and marketing activity has yielded additional challenges to those trying to understand the industry. Because few industry terms have been standardized, here is a list of terms as defined in this book.

- ✧ *Gourmet.* This guide uses the term *gourmet* sparingly, and as a synonym for "specialty."

- ✧ *Specialty food.* The National Association for the Specialty Food Trade has adopted the following description of specialty foods:

1

Specialty food products consist of foods, beverages, or confections meant for human use that are of the highest grade, style, and/or quality in their category. Their specialty nature derives from a combination of some or all of the following qualities: their uniqueness, exotic origin, particular processing, design, limited supply, unusual application or use, extraordinary packaging, or channel of distribution—the common denominator of which is their unusually high quality.

Specialty food is the traditionally accepted term meaning food products that fit the following criteria:

✧ *High quality*. Above all, the specialty food product must be of the highest quality, in both content and form. As a rule, only the best ingredients are used, whether the product is a premium ice cream or a mustard with peppercorns. Specialty food products sold at retail must also look the part—a high price demands that the product appears to be fancy and high tone.

✧ *High price*. Most specialty foods are priced higher than staple food products because of costly ingredients and labor used in their preparation. Others are high in cost because of high demand and limited supply. Still others are sold at high prices because of the low turnover they generate in retail stores (the longer they remain on the shelf, the more they cost the retailer).

✧ *Limited availability*. Many specialty foods have appeal because they are not generally available. Such foods often gain a cult status—fresh caviar is an example—in that they offer the consumer a cachet not offered by products sold everywhere.

✧ *Imported or unique*. Imported specialty foods no longer maintain a strong hold on the market. Many high quality products are now produced in this country and retain the "imported" distinction that first brought them to U.S. consumers' attention.

✧ *Food producer/processor.* The producer is usually the grower, and the processor is the one who adds value by processing the raw commodity into a table-ready food product.

✧ *Food broker.* A commissioned sales representative, usually with broad experience in the food industry, who generally calls mostly on distributors and large retail chains.

✧ *Specialty food distributor.* A company that buys in volume, for its own account, and sells to retailers (and to other distributors).

✧ *Store-door delivery.* Delivery made to stores by distributors.

✧ *Direct store distributor.* A distributor who performs many of the same services as a jobber (described in this section).

✧ *Wholesaler.* Companies that contract with, for example, a chain supermarket to warehouse and deliver a product that has been sold by the food producer to the supermarket. Wholesalers usually buy the product only when the producer has sold it to the supermarket chain. It is highly unlikely that you will have to deal with wholesalers because most of them are not equipped to handle the very detailed nature of specialty food merchandising.

✧ *Rack jobbers.* These are the people you see in supermarkets stocking shelves (they are the ones with the suits and ties, as opposed to supermarket employees). They price the incoming merchandise with price stickers (in those states where this is still required), fix shelf labels, follow schematic diagrams approved by the store, remove damaged and returned merchandise, and stock and dust the shelves.

✧ *Customers*. Retailers and distributors.

✧ *Consumers*. "Our reason for existing."

Identifying Your Primary Markets

Sales of specialty foods have tended to be concentrated in the more affluent market areas, both in the United States and abroad because of the relatively high retail prices involved. There are 40 primary U.S. trade areas of this type, and the majority of your prospective clients will fall within them (see Figure 1.1).

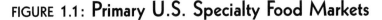

FIGURE 1.1: Primary U.S. Specialty Food Markets

This map of primary U.S. specialty food markets provides a visual representation that will assist you in directing your marketing efforts. Note that entire states can be virtually ignored during your initial introductory efforts.

A variety of different retail outlets have the potential to handle specialty food products. So-called gourmet shops are the most obvious, but there are also cheese shops, delicatessens, gift stores, and, in increasing numbers, supermarkets and department stores.

Supermarkets in the Midwest and Southwest have tended to play a stronger role in the specialty food trade than have supermarkets in other parts of the country. Their imported, ethnic, or specialty foods sections are often quite large and offer a diversified selection of items. As a corollary, gourmet shops are fewer in that region.

Many more supermarkets, especially independent chains, in all major trading areas have taken on so-called gourmet products. Over the past 15 years, some of the nation's largest supermarket chains, such as Safeway, Kroger, Vons, and Giant Foods have invested significantly in expanding their shelf space to carry specialty foods. Safeway, Vons, and Giant have opened separate specialty food stores. Safeway's are called Bon Appetit, Giant's are called Someplace Special, and Von's are called Von's Pavilions. Each offers a mix of high quality staples, "picture perfect" fresh produce, frozen foods, and specialty items. Another example is Busch's, an 11-store supermarket chain in Michigan, which owns and manages specialty food stores called Vic's World Class Markets. The industry is watching these ventures with an eye to adopting new directions in distributing specialty foods.

There are approximately 155,000 food stores in the United States, and only 25,000 of them can be considered prime prospects for specialty food products. This figure results from careful, conservative paring down of the raw data presented in business directories. The total of prime prospects is composed

> **CASE IN POINT**
>
> *Blanchard & Blanchard—The company started in 1984, and sold to new owners in 1989. Still Vermont-based and producing a line of salad dressings under the Blanchard label and marinades, ketchup, and cocktail sauces under the Vermont Epicurean label. Working on wider distribution with some success in grocery markets. Company also produces products for others (co-packing) under private labels. Suggests "having your own production facility allows for other revenue sources while introducing your own products." Stresses the importance of knowing your cost of goods.*

of approximately 4,800 gourmet shops, 7,300 cheese shops and health food stores, 7,500 delicatessens, and 3,400 chain supermarket outlets, gift shops, and major department stores.

It would be unlikely for you to reach all of these prime prospects without national distribution capability, either on your own, or through a major specialty food distributor.

In view of the "upscale" nature of specialty food product lines, using weighted rankings of *The New Yorker* magazine Selected Marketing System can identify primary marketing targets. This identifies and ranks markets for quality, premium-priced products, rather than simply ranking markets by total population and income data.

The 40 primary trade areas listed in Figure 1.2 are the most important United States markets for quality merchandise.

FIGURE 1.2: Primary Trade Areas (in order of primacy)

New York	San Diego	Hartford
Los Angeles	Denver	New Orleans
Chicago	Baltimore	Sacramento
San Francisco	Atlanta	Columbus
Detroit	Pittsburgh	Indianapolis
Washington, D.C.	St. Louis	Oklahoma City
Philadelphia	Phoenix	San Antonio
Houston	Milwaukee	Salt Lake City
Boston	Portland	Charlotte
Miami/Fort Lauderdale	Kansas City	Allentown/Bethlehem
Dallas/Fort Worth	Riverside/San Bernardino	Buffalo
Seattle-Tacoma	Cincinnati	West Palm Beach
Cleveland-Akron	Honolulu	
Minneapolis-St. Paul	Tampa/St. Petersburg	

About 15,000 of the 23,000 prime prospects are located in these areas. The listing is an accurate reflection of the trade in general. Although a strictly specialty food ranking would include all of those listed, the order in which they are listed would be somewhat different.

Segmenting Your Markets

Our identification of geographic/demographic markets for specialty food represents one of the first elements of the marketing process. Matters of consumer preference, ethnic division, population movement, taste, and historical trends further segment these markets.

To illustrate, hot and spicy foods have long been accepted in the Southwest, whereas, they have recently gained a strong foothold in New England markets. In Southern California, everybody eats outdoors where the barbecue and barbecue products reign! And it is difficult to introduce a new product to Floridians in the summer when specialty food business tends to fall off drastically.

Health Food Stores

The mounting importance of health food stores should be taken into account. According to the market research firm, Packaged Facts, natural and health food sales were expected to climb more than 10 percent annually through 1999, when they will approach $8 billion. Distribution channels for health foods differ in some cases. Some distributors carry only health food lines, while others only service the more upscale channels of distribution (e.g., fancy gourmet food stores). There are profitable opportunities to be explored in this segment of the industry if your product meets its criteria.

The Gift Trade

The gift trade is also playing a greater part in specialty food marketing, partly due to the widespread use of slotting fees in regular food distribution channels. There are more than 70,000 gift or gift-type stores in the entire country. This figure includes both upscale and standard outlets. As with health food stores, distribution channels can differ in that segment.

The food rep (broker) who maintains a showroom, attends and exhibits at gift shows, and calls extensively on retail accounts serves much of the gift trade. Such brokers are paid a 15 percent

commission of the invoice value of all sales to retailers made in accordance with the broker contract.

An overall understanding of these differing market segments and varying distribution requirements will be helpful to you as you plan your marketing and distribution strategy.

Military Exchanges

If you can make the right connection, the Army and Air Force Exchange System, the Navy Exchange, and the commissaries (military supermarkets) offer interesting possibilities for substantial sales. These stores serve the military families located in many parts of the world. Such families have many of the same needs and wants as do families in any of the major continental U.S. trade areas. I have seen a wide assortment of fancy and specialty foods available at these outlets.

Ethnic Foods

For our purposes, ethnic foods means retail and food-service packaged food products that can be described generally as either Italian, Hispanic, Kosher, Oriental, or Greek. A variation of this is the so-called fusion style. A key fusion-style trend exists in Asian and Pan-Asian foods wherein one might encounter dishes made of combined food and flavor types from Thailand, Japan, China, Vietnam, and Indonesia.

Italian-style foods comprise one of the largest categories, and Italian ingredients have become one of the basics of our everyday cuisine. Because of this, there is an enormous market for Italian foods. But, is there room for another pasta or olive oil?

The United States is said to be the fifth largest Spanish-speaking country in the world. Our Hispanic population exceeds 24 million and is the fastest growing consumer market. The best products for growth will be staples advertised and promoted in

> ### CASE IN POINT
> *Mr. and Mrs. "T" Bloody Mary Mix—A big hit, first introduced by Taylor Foods. Now the brand is owned by Heublein and marketed everywhere. This is a successful example of a transition product.*

Spanish by the major food producer/processors. Your opportunity will lie in the growing interest in Hispanic and Hispanic-style foods and cooking.

The Kosher food market exceeded $3.5 billion in 1999, and it is expected to continue its ten percent plus annual growth. The broad appeal of Kosher foods beyond that which is mandated by Jewish dietary practice is based on the quality associated with such foods. More than 75 percent of Kosher food consumers are non-Jewish. In order to be certified Kosher, a food product must pass an exacting inspection by an authorized Rabbinical agency.

American consumer interest in health and fitness has spurred growth of foods that are unprocessed and fresh. This includes a great number of Oriental foods. The market for this category exceeds $1 billion at retail. Among the leading Oriental food products are vegetables, sauces, and dry mixes. Increasing home use of stir-fry is also encouraging Oriental food consumption. Today, once exotic foods such as ginger root, Oriental vegetables, tempura sauce, and bean sprouts are readily available.

Greek foods, also referred to as Mediterranean cuisine, are growing in popularity because of their traditional reliance on freshness. Some examples include olive oil, cheese, honey, dressings, and baked goods. A most notable addition to these examples is humus. Four years ago, most people didn't have a clue what it was. It could only be found in specialty food stores, but now it is found as a staple in supermarkets. It has leapt virtually from entirely ethnic markets to mainstream society.

Your opportunity with the ethnic food category may be twofold: (1) produce and market traditional ethnic food products not otherwise available to consumers, and/or (2) market new "ethnic-style" products to both ethnic and "non-ethnic" consumers.

CASE IN POINT

On the costs, perils, and pitfalls of specialty food marketing, Barbara Henry, President of Bogland (producers of a full line of cranberry-based chutney, mustard, grill sauce, vinaigrette, marmalade, and blueberry preserves) has this to say, "Before you begin, don't quit your day job, don't quit your night job. Think about it . . . think about it again . . . then, wait six months and think about it once more." Sound advice from an entrepreneur whose company started selling BJ's Colonial mustard in 1987 and now has a full line of gourmet condiments with a growing national distribution.

Taking Advantage of Export Markets

The following quotation comes from a guide to commercial food production: "The last thing you should consider . . . is the potential for overseas marketing of your product."

That kind of thinking forms the basis of why the United States has failed so miserably in capturing profitable food marketing opportunities overseas. Aside from the product-oriented nature of U.S. food marketing, this kind of narrow-minded approach simply opens the door to foreign competition.

Instead of just looking in your own backyard, try, instead, to identify the world markets where your product would have the greatest comparative advantage. It may be that, indeed, your region in the states is the best place for you to start. There are, however, lots of reasons to consider non-traditional markets. There is a commonality in food marketing, regardless of the market. Despite language and taste differences, you can profit from exploring markets abroad. Ask your State Department of Agriculture and the U.S. Foreign Agricultural Service for information about current promotional support. This includes trade shows and other overseas market development services. Also, contact the National Association for the Specialty Food Trade (NASFT), which sponsored its own pavilion at Salon International de Alimentation (SIAL) in Paris in 2000.

Initially, your primary overseas markets will be the major trade areas in Canada, Europe, and Japan, with potential in Latin America and the Middle East. See Chapter 3: "Taking Your Product to Market."

Going for the Big Win with Transition Products

Many specialty food producers are attracted to the idea that their product will capture public imagination and sell like crazy. They envision the day when everyone will beat a path to their door demanding their product! When, and if, this happens (and it can happen), the product will reach a transition stage from up-market specialty food distribution to down-market grocery trade.

In some markets, your product will continue to be merchandised as a specialty item, while in others, it will be sold solely on grocery/supermarket shelves.

Recent examples of transition products include Perrier Water, Grey Poupon Mustard, Red Oval Stoned Wheat Thins, Cadbury Chocolate Bars, and Häagen-Dazs Ice Cream.

Understanding Gourmet Store Concerns

Your understanding of how your product is merchandised (placed before the consumer in the retail store) will influence the direction of all your marketing efforts. Figure 1.3 shows some of the types of classifications of specialty food stores. Having some knowledge of how a typical retail gourmet food store operates will enable you to work more effectively with your distributors, brokers, and the store manager. Figure 1.4 illustrates the product mix an average store may carry.

Average Opening Costs for a 1,000-Square-Foot Store	
Leasehold, improvements	$50,000
Equipment	35,000
Start-up	15,000
Inventory	15,000
Total	$115,000

Product selection will depend on store type and on a variety of demographic conditions. Certain food products are in higher demand in certain regions. If you are selling your version of a hot salsa, then you will probably have better luck by introducing it to New England fancy food stores than to those in the Southwest, where a "million" such products are well established in grocery distribution.

FIGURE 1.3: **Specialty Food Store Classifications**

Type	Classification
Upscale deli	Delicatessen foods and associated condiments.
Specialty	Gourmet foods, sometimes with specific upscale product lines (coffee, for example).
Cheese	All kinds of cheese and related items.
Gift	Gift baskets.
Housewares	Gourmet pots and pans and other cookware, with some impulse and companion food items.
Department	Upscale with heavy emphasis on cookware and some confectionery. (Demonstrations play a key role in cookware sales.)
General	Combination of all of the above, including some traditional staples.

FIGURE 1.4: **Product Mix in a Gourmet Store**

The average gourmet store generally sells a mix of products along the following lines:

Product Line	Approximate Percentage of Sales
Condiments	40
Beverages (including bottled water)	5
Coffee and tea	5
Cheese	5
Pâtés and meats	10
Prepared foods	15
Confection	10
Other	10
	100%

As a rule, the manager of a small specialty food store will work very long hours, in effect "marrying" the store. Many of the most successful retail specialty food enterprises are operated by families—for obvious reasons. You may be interested in knowing how the "average" manager spends her/his time:

8 AM to Noon	Ordering/opening/training Food preparation
Noon to 2 PM	Luncheon sales
2 PM to 7 PM	General administration/baking supplier meetings (this is you)

Your role is to operate for the convenience of the retailer, who, in turn, operates for the convenience of the consumer.

Your Role as Supplier

The Boston Consulting Group, a company involved in the purchase, sale, and management of restaurants and retail gourmet food stores suggests the following guidelines:

✧ *Become involved.* Get to know the particular challenges confronting each key retailer.

✧ *Educate the buyer.* Provide point-of-purchase materials. Arrange to spend some time with the sales staff.

✧ *Follow-up on deliveries.* Determine if all went well.

✧ *Follow-up on shortages.* Ascertain if still needed and fill orders.

✧ *Develop seasonal guidelines.* Find out what works best, where.

✧ *Agree to minimum orders.* Be prepared to "break" cases.

✧ *Try to allow exclusivity.* Try not to sell same product to competitor across the street.

Understanding the Specialty Food Consumer

A good resource for learning more about the specialty food consumer is NASFT. In 1999, NASFT produced a series of reports on the demographics of the specialty food consumer. NASFT gathered data from market research sources and combined some 20 specialty food brands into one list, and then compared them with the demographics of consumers who purchased those products.

Topics about specialty food consumers covered in the research included the following (as an example, I have appended results to each category that show the likelihood of each demographic segment to purchase specialty foods):

Demographic	Most Likely to Purchase
With whom they live	Two persons
How much they earn	$50,000–$74,999
How old they are	35–44
Their racial background	White
Age of children	No children
Home owners or renters	Owners
Level of formal education	College graduate
Where they live (census division)	Pacific and South Atlantic

The report continues with an in-depth discussion of the specialty food consumer lifestyles and provides data about the specialty cookie consumer, specialty tea consumer, and specialty chocolate consumer.

CHAPTER TWO

Getting Ready to Market

This chapter considers the importance of vision, understanding your business as part of a system, customer needs, start-up costs, consumer demand, and the market research required before you undertake a large production run for your product. The chapter also examines product categories in demand, and it addresses the issues of producing, packaging, labeling, and pricing your product. A description of warehousing, inventory, and shipping is included, and, finally the role of the Internet in specialty food marketing is addressed.

The Importance of Vision

Long-term success all boils down to how we can better relate to one another. It is a new way of doing business, one that is customer-directed, process-oriented, and in which decisions are based on facts. No longer is long-term success assured by wholly intuitive, seat-of-the-pants marketing.

Of course, there have been, and always will be, exceptions to prove this rule. In the food business, these will be based usually on products that are in high demand—ones that consumers will do or pay anything to get—or those that are associated with, and introduced by, marketers with deep pockets. Even then, if the product does not meet a specific consumer need at the right quality and right price, it will be short lived.

We can no longer simply afford to think up a new food product, prepare it, and try to market it. Instead use the information from Figure 2.1 to focus your efforts.

How does all this connect to the food entrepreneur? How does the entrepreneur, wearing all the hats at once, maintain focus? The answer is VISION. Simply put, your vision is what you envision yourself being (as food entrepreneur, professional, spouse, parent, neighbor, citizen, etc.) in about five to ten years. It is your dream. As a food entrepreneur, your vision should be a positive and inspiring statement of where your business will be at that time. A clearly articulated vision will help you and all your stakeholders (anyone with an interest in your venture) keep on track. Important elements of your organizational vision might include: reputation, products to offer, values, types of customer, working environment, manner in which your people would work together, and how you and your team would handle both good and bad times.

You will want to share your dream with, and solicit input from, these stakeholders if you are to develop the appropriate response. Revisit your vision from time to time. See how it can be constantly refined. Your vision will help you determine if the task or activity you are doing now is adding value to getting from where you are, to where you ENVISION yourself being in five or ten years.

What you are doing, or about to do in food marketing, is part of a system. This system consists of inputs, actions, and outputs. If you can develop the right supplier partnering (inputs), understand variation in your process (actions), and be able to set

FIGURE 2.1: Checklist to Refine Your Focus

What to Do	How to Do It
1. Identify prospective customers (retailers, distributors, etc.).	Visit stores where like products are sold; attend food-related trade shows; contact NASFT and regional food trade associations; contact state associations/agencies.
2. Determine customer needs (distinguish between customer and consumer needs).	Consumers are the ultimate users of your product. They will determine the quality of your product; retailers and distributors will determine the quality of your service. Each category has specific needs. Survey them to determine the quality characteristics of their specific needs.
3. Prepare a product in response to those needs.	Many of you most likely already have a product in mind. Make sure it conforms with your findings in number 2 above.
4. Test the product (trade shows are good vehicles for this).	This is extremely important. Test for taste acceptance, label and packaging effect, etc. Make sure your product meets, or exceeds, your customer's needs.
5. Refine the product based on data from the tests (change flavor, size, container, labels, etc.).	There will ALWAYS be room for improvement.
6. Return to number 2, repeat the cycle.	This process is the basis of what we call the PDCA cycle: Plan, Do, Check, and Act.

measurable quality standards (outputs), you have a substantially greater chance of delighting your customer.

To delight your customers, everyone involved must devote sufficient time to education and training in developing a quality philosophy. This is probably the most difficult part of this process . . . taking assets away from what we do best—fire fighting—and focusing them on long-term thinking.

The point. Food marketing, and the business supporting it, cannot continue in the same vein as it has in the past. The food industry is notoriously product-driven. We are being snookered out of profit-generating opportunities because we lack vision— a vision based on perceived customer quality standards. Make the bold move. Cut the waste. Set aside a half-hour or more each week to think about your vision. See if the path you have selected is headed in the desired direction.

Your vision is just one of the important elements to consider in your continuous improvement effort. Another way to put it: Think of your vision as you dream about the future. Other elements include the mission (what you do to realize your vision), guiding principles (standards of how you do business, your values and goals), and strategic objectives.

Assumption. You want to develop, produce, administer, market, and sell food that is valued and wanted by customers. As the quality of your work improves, so does your productivity. And, costs go down. Knowing how to effect this requires knowing something about Continuous Process Improvement. The term is self-explanatory. All of the processes you want to improve all the time are part of a system. What you do as a food entrepreneur should be understood in context of this system.

Your system consists of:

> ✦ *Inputs.* Customer needs/feedback, ingredients, packaging materials, trained employees, etc.

✧ *Food processing.* What you do to formulate and prepare your food product (your response to the customer need).

✧ *Outputs.* The packaged, labeled, priced, and positioned product.

✧ *Outcomes.* Many satisfied repeat customers (or the opposite).

Managing your system and putting this all into perspective necessitates developing your company's Vision, Mission, Guiding Principles, and Strategic Goals and Objectives.

Vision helps the food entrepreneur maintain focus and inspire employee loyalty and dedication.

A Vision Example: [by the year 2010] "Our company is internationally recognized as the premier supplier of [your food products]. We continue to provide innovative [your food products] that provide value and regularly exceed customer expectations."

Why Do I Need to Think about a Mission?

Once you have articulated and shared your Vision with everyone in your firm, you will need to figure out what you are going to do to realize it. The result is called your Mission.

How to Develop a Mission Statement

The first and last rule is to know your customer. This presumes that you have people who want to buy and consume your food. It also presumes that you know something about your customer's needs. This information is then compared with your "bag of tricks"—your distinctive creative and production capabilities—that you utilize to formulate a response to the perceived customer needs. This process can be accomplished by brainstorming ideas.

Brainstorming Is a Useful Tool

Organize your *mission team*. This should consist of five to seven members from various "departments" in your company. As a small business, this might be everyone. Gather them for a brainstorming session. Brainstorming involves each member and encourages open thinking. There are a variety of brainstorming types. We suggest the following (from *The Team Handbook*, pp. 2–38 to 2–39, published by Joiner Associates, Inc.):

Rules for conducting a brainstorming session are as follows:

✧ Encourage everyone to freewheel; don't hold back on any ideas, even if they seem silly at the time; the more ideas the better.

✧ No discussion during brainstorm. That will come later.

✧ Let people hitchhike—build upon ideas generated by others in the group.

✧ Write ALL ideas on a flipchart so the whole group can easily scan them.

The general sequence of events in a brainstorm is to

✧ review the topic, defining the subject of the brainstorm. Often this is done best as a "why," or "what" question. ("What are possible ways to inform and train supervisors and hourly workers on all three shifts?" "How can we get all the information we need on a regular basis to complete these forms on time?")

✧ give everyone a minute or two of silence to think about the question.

✧ invite everyone to call out his or her ideas. The meeting facilitator should enforce the ground rules ("No discussion! Next idea . . .").

✧ have one team member write down all ideas on the flipchart, pausing only to check accuracy.

Feel free to modify this procedure to fit the group and the topic. For instance, you could have everyone write down their ideas, then go around the group and have each person say one of their ideas, continuing in this way until everyone's list is complete. Or you could do the entire sequence in stages: first, have everyone think of the minimal or partial solutions to a problem followed by the most outrageous, unconventional, or expensive solutions; then try to meld the two together into reasonable alternatives. Be particularly alert for ways to combine suggestions.

CASE IN POINT

Beth's Fine Desserts—For the past 11 years, this company's principal has considered herself a baker and an artist. Feels all food entrepreneurs need to "Fix their vision," which, in her case, is to be on the shelf next to Pepperidge Farm and Sara Lee. Beyond that, she feels that success is a combination of inner peace and happiness. It took about six years for the company to be successful. Beth suggests seed money of at least $50K, better at $100K.

Brainstorming will help you define your mission and will clarify how you will go about meeting, even exceeding, perceived customer needs and expectations. This is your mission. It's what you do, the nature of your business.

A mission example. My company produces the best [your food products] that offer outstanding value, and result in regular and repeat sales. We do this in a working environment that is customer-oriented and in which our employees are fully involved team members. We make decisions based on facts. We continually plan, track, and measure performance. Our mission success is every employee's business. Management relies on team members—who know the work better than anyone else does—to tell management how to help do the job better. We strive to produce the right product, the first time, and every time, at a price both our customer and we can afford.

A clearly defined organizational mission will go a long way in building your employees' pride, dedication, and team effort. The key to this is to organize for quality.

Determining Start-Up Costs

Here's an important piece of advice that is based on 20 years of gourmet food sales and marketing experience: You must have an independent source of income to successfully start your own gourmet food marketing business! You should have sufficient capital available to cover all your costs for the first three to five years. This includes all normal living expenses.

Your start-up costs will depend on your circumstances and on the type of product you plan to market. And even in light of such information, your specific start-up costs will be difficult to peg. As you will see in the following pages, our estimate ranges

from $35,000 to $100,000 per year for the first three years.

If you will be using your own kitchen facility, you can save money until your production requirements outstrip your kitchen's capability. After that, you will want to negotiate with a food packer/processor to have your product produced to meet the increased demand. The same goes for other overhead and administrative costs. You should take advantage of existing office space and equipment, and you might be able to use friends to help out part time.

Cost Elements of New Product Introduction by a Major Producer

Element	Percent of Costs
Advertising and consumer promotion*	46
Trade deals and allowances	16
Market research and product development	18
Other	20

*This means mostly promotions, such as mailing, trade show exhibition, in-store tastings, etc.

Source: "Managing the Process of Introducing and Deleting Products in the Grocery and Drug Industry," *Joint Industry Task Force*, 1990. Grocery Manufacturers of America, Inc.

The people referred to in scenarios two and three, at the beginning of this book, had offices, production facilities, and administrative capability. They were also operating an existing business.

Start-up costs encompass production, packaging, warehousing, administration, and product advertising and promotion costs. The specific cost categories include those listed in the accompanying "Guidelines for Success."

The data in the table on this page gives you an idea of cost elements used by the major leaguers. They cover costs of obtaining nationwide grocery distribution of warehouse-sourced products, and they do not include costs of direct-store delivered items.

✧ GUIDELINES FOR SUCCESS ✧

Start-Up Cost Analysis

Use these guides to determine your start-up costs.

Item	Cost Savings Considerations	Monthly Cost Estimate
Postage	Almost all of your mail will be first class. If you plan to do a lot of mail-order selling, then ask the post office for information about postage-paid and bulk mail privileges.	$100
Travel	You can reduce your travel costs by carefully planning your itinerary. Expect to make no more than four sales calls per day. Use a telephone whenever possible.	$600
Office supplies	You will need a computer (Pentium processor with a minimum of 500MHZ, 10 GB hard drive and 32 MB RAM, plus word processing, spreadsheet, database, and accounting software), laser printer, forms, bond paper, file cabinets, etc.	$300
Promotion	Business cards, catalog sheets, price lists, neck tags, point-of-purchase materials (possibly). Prepare your own press releases, at first. Do not advertise to the consumer unless you do mail-order. Restrict trade ads to a complete—well-managed—promo campaign. Otherwise, save your money to make sales calls.	$600
Telephone	If you do any trade advertising, for example, the telephone company will require you to install a business, instead of personal, line. Look into the cost of an 800-number (for your fax, too). Also, if you are on the road a lot, a cellular phone will be invaluable.	$250

Guidelines for Success, continued

Item	Cost Savings Considerations	Monthly Cost Estimate
Fax	Add a fax/voice mail modem (internal or external) with the appropriate software to your computer, and buy a regular fax machine.	$75
Utilities	Prorate your current utility cost (in your home) to cover that used by the business (if office in home).	$75
Rent	If your office is to be in your home, take a percentage of your monthly mortgage equal to the space occupied by your office. That will be your monthly rent.	$900
Product ingredients	Try to arrange minimum bulk shipments. Ask your supplier(s) to store the ingredients and to invoice you only when you draw down supply.	Product dependent
Product packaging	Find other companies that are producing a product in a container similar to yours. Try to realize economies of scale by ordering a large quantity and splitting the shipment between, or among, the other companies.	Product dependent
Labels	Labeling by hand during your initial stage will save you money. It will also allow you to experiment with different labels without having to order 10,000 of one kind, only to find out they won't work. You will require the talents of a good graphic artist.	Product dependent
Miscellaneous	All the rest. Figure about 10 percent of total costs.	Product dependent

Guidelines for Success, continued

Notes to Start-Up Cost Analysis

These monthly costs do not include cost of labor, most of which will be borne by you. Other costs of production, including inventory management, site selection, and quality control should be considered if you will be establishing your own production facility. Also, the rent figure ($900 per month) can be deferred, since it will be you paying yourself. The same goes for utilities.

The office supplies include initial purchase of a computer, word processing and related software, telephone answering machine (or voice messaging service), printer, adding machine, etc. The conservative, annualized, figure is $2,900. You may be able to do better with used or something other than top-of-the-line equipment.

The grand total, not including production (ingredients, packaging, labeling, and labor) or miscellaneous, comes to just over $34,800. This allows approximately $8,000 to $75,000 to cover the production element, bringing the estimated total dollar requirements to between $24,800 and $100,000 for each of the first three years.

Your cost percentages will be lower in advertising and consumer promotion, while higher by about 15 percent in the trade deals and allowances segment. In the end, trade advertising, promotion, and deals will constitute the major portion of your costs.

How Long Does It Take and How Much Does It Cost?

Producers Respond

Some of the following companies have gone on to other pursuits, but their responses remain valid:

Chautauqua Hills Jelly Company packs and distributes jams, jellies, and chocolate sauces. The company started with $100,000, but would have preferred $150,000. It recommends $100,000 to $150,000 per year for three to five years for success, and submits the following as a *successful specialty food product line: Pasta Mamma's gourmet pasta and sauces.*

Pasta Mamma's derives some of its revenue base from a 2,500 square foot retail food business. It produces and sells fresh, dried, flavored gourmet pasta and sauces. It has been in business four years, and reports that it can take three to five years before success can be attained. "The amount of money required depends on the attitude and focus of the owner/manager who must be willing to listen, follow-up, and make cold sales calls."

The Herb Patch Ltd. has spent the past 16 years producing instant cocoa mixes, flavored honeys, salt-free culinary blends, herbal teas, and vinegars. It names the following as examples of successful specialty food products: Honey Acres (honey and honey mustard), Jardines Foods (full line of Texas foods), and Maple Grove (pure maple syrup and maple syrup products).

Pelican Bay Ltd. says it could not afford the start-up costs if it started today. The company produces and markets unique blends of all natural herbs and spices for dips, seasonings, drink mixes, and mixes for children. It advises that it would take upwards of five years for a new entrant to succeed.

Peachtree Specialty Foods has produced an extensive line of condiments and sauces for the past three years. The company was sold in 1995 to a Williamsburg, Virginia specialty foods concern. The line has high quality ingredients and packaging; and they exhibit in many trade shows. The owner recommends newcomer stakes of $25,000 to $30,000 per year get into this industry.

North Aire Market won the 1995 NASFT Outstanding Pasta, Beans, and Rice Award for their "Prairie Blaze

Popcorn." North Aire started in 1987, and they now consider themselves successful. When asked about their start-up costs a partner responded: "It is not success in terms of money expanded, but in terms of close relationships held fast." She and her partner have remained on good terms throughout.

Goldwater's Foods of Arizona, Inc. markets Goldwater's "Taste of the Southwest," Sedona Red Salsas, Paradise Pineapple Salsa, and Rio Verde Tomatillo Salsa. It recommends beginners invest $250,000 over a seven-year period to succeed. They propose the following as a successful specialty food product line: Peggy-Jane's Salad Dressing (now marketed by Knotts Berry Farm).

Grace Tea Company, Ltd. distributes Grace Rare Teas. The company principal says: "With regards to money, it is best to try to use someone else's." He advises entrants to raise $100,000 to $150,000 per year for the first six years to succeed.

Golden Walnut Specialty Food has been marketing specialty foods for ten years. It sells Golden Walnut cookies, shortbread Almond Ingot cakes, and cheesecakes; and they report they are operating in the black. When asked about the specialty food market, the company principal comments that he was "very surprised at how complex and competitive it is."

Harney & Sons, Ltd. distributes Connoisseur fine teas. This company is a focused, niche player. It began by selling only to institutional accounts (mostly hotels and private clubs) through personal networking. The owner points out that the amount of money to succeed depends

CASE IN POINT

Mendocino Mustards—Began 25 years ago as one mustard line and on a part-time basis. The product was well received in California. Seventeen years later, they introduced their second product. The owners believe they are successful because their mustard is so widely accepted in California. No clue as to how much it costs to reach success.

Vision: Their mustards are the number-one best selling, all natural, high quality mustards in the United States.

on too many variables to pin down, and suggests that success for a beginner will take at least three years.

Ridley's Muffin Chips produced its initial revenues from a retail muffin store. Demand for their leftover muffin pieces grew so fast that product was reformulated into a muffin chip. This one is a success. They made a product hit from a mistake.

Researching the Market to Identify Consumer Demand

One of your first and most important forays into the marketplace will be to determine the strength of demand for your product. You will also want to see who else is marketing a similar product (the competition), at what price, in what packaging, and with what sort of promotional support.

Weigh the following market research considerations and keep your findings in mind as you make your production, packaging, labeling, pricing, inventory, and shipping arrangements. Explore the issues of how the industry works and acquire information that will provide you with a solid foundation about

✧ major participants.

✧ recent trends.

✧ prospects for a product such as yours.

✧ technical and production requirements.

✧ regulatory influence (food and drug laws).

✧ competitive situation.

✧ industry advertising and promotion methods.

Be prepared to gather as much information and data as possible about the potential for your product. Do not underestimate the value of networking. A lot of specialty food producers and marketers will be happy to share their experiences and insights with you. If they can't answer your question, then ask them for the names of three other participants who might be able to respond.

✦ GUIDELINES FOR SUCCESS ✦
Market Research

What to Do	How to Do It
Define and analyze the specialty foods industry.	Visit major specialty food industry trade shows, especially those sponsored by NASFT.
Identify industry participants: producers, distributors, brokers, retailers, and consumers.	Visit shows and review this guide. Gather information from the NASFT.
Develop overview of major trends. Understand current changes in consumer requirements for specialty foods, in general, and for the food category you have in mind, in particular.	Review industry trade journals (see Appendix A).
Describe important suppliers, especially those with whom you will be competing. Understand the various sales, marketing, and distribution strategies they employ.	Visit food shows. Ask questions. Take notes.
Review impact of technology on the entire marketing process, including production, packaging, and order processing. What are the technological implications for your application?	For example, will your ingredients require special machinery to process? Will the package you have selected require special orders from high-tech packaging companies? Contact the Institute of Food Technologies, 221 N. LaSalle St., Chicago, IL 60601 312-782-8424.

Guidelines for Success, continued

What to Do	How to Do It
Describe regulatory influence on the production, packaging, labeling, and marketing of your intended product.	Check your state's regulations and FDA for sanitary certification. Check Chapter 21 of the Code of Federal Regulations (CFR) for labeling and ingredient statements. Most states prohibit the use of your own kitchen; a separate facility is required.

Developing Your Product

Marketing strategies will differ depending on whether your product is fresh, refrigerated, or frozen. Also, matters of shelf life—the time it takes for your product to deteriorate—will have to be considered. For example, chocolate products are traditionally sold and shipped during cooler seasons. Otherwise, the cost of shipping can escalate and place your chocolate product out of the competition. A product with a short shelf life will have to move off the shelf faster. To ensure this may require a considerable promotional expenditure.

A comprehensive market profile appears in Appendix O. The profile discusses major specialty food product categories in terms of configuration, types, recent trends, size, market share, and other considerations. You will find it useful to review the category in which you hold an interest in order to become better informed about your prospects for success.

An ever-changing list of upscale products rated with the highest growth potential appears as Figure 2.2. The products with the least potential for growth are in Figure 2.3. Those products with the greatest growth potential tend to be high-quality, convenient foods. They are foods that are perceived, for the most part, as being healthy, or healthier than others, while offering the benefit of a special treat.

FIGURE 2.2: **Upscale Products with the Greatest Growth Potential**

Appetizers/hors d'oeuvres

Candy

Cereals

Coffee

Chocolate

Crackers

Beverages

Value added meat/poultry

Bottled water

Fruit

Fancy mustards

Exotic mushrooms

Ice cream/sorbet

Non-alcoholic beverages

Nuts

Pasta

Oils/vinegars

Seafood

Salsa/hot sauces

Pâté

Goat cheese (chèvre)

Salad dressings

Sauces/bases

Juices

Seasonings/spices/herbs

Tea

Breads

Cakes/pastry

Vegetables (and beans)

FIGURE 2.3: **Upscale Products with the Least Growth Potential**

Alcoholic beverages

Soups

Syrups/honey

Dessert toppings

Jams/jellies and preserves

Rice

Condiments (except certain sauces,
    mustards, and salsas)

There are all kinds of exceptions to the above listings. For example, almost any food that claims it is organic is probably carving out a profitable niche. Other "hot" aspects include genetically modified organisms, soy, organic, orange, and smoky foods. Also, even though alcoholic beverages appear to be on the wane, there has been a mushrooming of so-called microbreweries. Such brands as Ommegang Brewery's Rare VOS Belgian-style beer is just one such exception. The Stonewall Kitchen line of jams and preserves is another exception, in this case to the slower growing jams/jellies and preserves category.

> **CASE IN POINT**
>
> *The Infamous Cookie was exhibited by Duchess Farms Company at the 1977 National Fancy Food and Confection Show in New Orleans. Its packaging featured the comment "sinfully good," with the likeness of actor Vincent Price. This was a potentially winning combination. Where are the cookies today? The excellent product positioning apparently was not backed up with the required funding.*

Positioning Your Product

The term *product positioning* covers the overall concept of how your product will be marketed. It includes pricing, packaging, labeling, advertising, and promotion considerations. For example, a Cajun-style food might better be positioned as a gift/souvenir, when sold in New Orleans, than merely as a food product. It would be positioned in such a way as to attract attention of tourists. Successful positioning has to do with your best assessment of what benefit you will be providing to your prospective consumer. How to appeal to this consumer is the point of product positioning.

There are many examples. Who knew that bottled water would make such headway in the United States? Our tap water is supposed to be perfectly safe and wholly acceptable for all of our water needs. Then, in the 1970s, Source Perrier invested an estimated $3 million to position its bottled water as an alternative to tap water, and, even more importantly, as an alternative to alcohol in bars and restaurants. Perrier is bottled in a unique container, imported from France, and it commands a higher price than its competition. Yet it has developed an impressive lead in its market . . . all by effective product positioning. The point of positioning is to differentiate your product.

Everyone knows about the apple. Yes, it is healthy. Yes, it is inexpensive. Yes, it is available at every grocery in the nation. So, if you have a new "apple," then you will have to differentiate it from the others. Doing this is called product positioning. Think hard about novel means of packaging and promoting it. Remember the Pet Rock? Read "Pliskin's Phables," which follows, for an effective and amusing description of product positioning.

Pliskin's Phables
How Positioning Began

(With thanks to Mr. Pliskin)

In the beginning, the woman Eve was shopping in the Garden of Eden. As she was browsing through the fresh produce section, a serpent appeared unto her. "Psst, woman!" said the Serpent, "try this." "What is it, O Serpent?" asked Eve. And the Serpent spake unto her, "It is a fruit, as yet unnamed. It grows on the tree of paradise, and it's mostly roughage, so it's good for what aileth you. And, it's a product of nature: 85 percent water, vitamins A and C, calcium, thiamin, riboflavin, iron, and niacin." "I've never heard of vitamins," said Eve, "but I don't aileth. I feel great." "Try a bite. Just a bite," urged the Serpent, holding an apple toward her. "It's just what you needeth." "Who needeth anything that's good for them?" retorted Eve, as she headed for the heavenly hash ice cream. "Curses!" spake the Serpent unto himself. "I was sure she'd fall for it." And he slithered away to thinketh. "I know I've got a great product here. Yea, verily, the projected sales figures are out of this world. Maybe my segmentation aileth. Maybe I barketh up the wrong tree. Hmmmeth. Hallelujah! The woman Eve is also a mother. Maybe this product is for kids!"

And so the Serpent hired unto him a $100,000-a-year-copy-writer. And this copywriter delivered unto the Serpent a terrific advertising slogan: "An apple a day keepeth the doctor away."... And the Serpent saw it was good. The next day, when Eve was shopping, the Serpent appeared unto her again. "Psst, Mom!" said the Serpent, "try this!" "What is it?" asked Eve. "It's a fruit named apple," said the Serpent. "Your kids are gonna love it. It's a sweet, crunchy fun food. Great for afterschool quicketh energy!" "Forget it," said Eve. "Cain and Abel have enough energy. They're killing each other already!" "But," said the Serpent, "it is written: An apple a day keepeth the doctor away." "Who needeth a doctor in paradise?" said Eve. "Besides, my kids eateth only peanut butter and jelly." "Double curses!" hissed the Serpent, and he crawled off to thinketh again. He thought and he thought and he thought. And his thinking begat an idea. He decided to undertaketh giant systematic research. First he spake unto consumers in Kansas City, Rochester, and Des Moines. And they spake unto him of their desires. Then he called in Yankelovich to checketh the demographics. And Yankelovich spake unto the truth of the Serpent's findings in a 16-volume report. Then he handed the word of Yankelovich over to a new-product consulting firm, and he awaited their suggestions. And those of the firm spake unto him of the target market and communications thereto, and the Serpent did as he was told. He painted the apple bright red. He polished it until it shone even as the sun. He garnished it with a stem and a little green leaf.... And he saw it was good. Then he placed it in the center of the fruit section and crawled off to waiteth. The next day, the woman Eve came byeth pushing her shopping cart. The beautiful apple caught her eye, and she spake. "O Serpent," she asked, "what's this?" And the Serpent knew great joy, and he spake unto her, "It's something new. It's a tempting dessert. It's a little sinful, and all natural, and very,

> **CASE IN POINT**
>
> *One Product versus Multi-Product Line—Unless you have a truly extraordinary product, it is very difficult to introduce a one-product line. Exceptions to this include: Tabasco Sauce, Grey Poupon Dijon Mustard, and A-1 Sauce, all of which required years to develop any kind of brand position.*

very indulgent, and loweth in calories and it's called 'Fatal Apple.' You probably can't afford it." "Sayeth who?" said Eve, "I'll take a bushel." And lo, the Serpent and Eve begat positioning, which dwelleth among us, even unto this day.

Carving Out Your Share of Market

Market share is the percentage of a given market that a food producer is said to control. For example, XYZ Tea Company may claim a 75 percent share of the market for "imported retail packaged British tea." This means that of all the retail packaged British Tea sold in the U.S., 75 percent is sold by XYZ Tea Company.

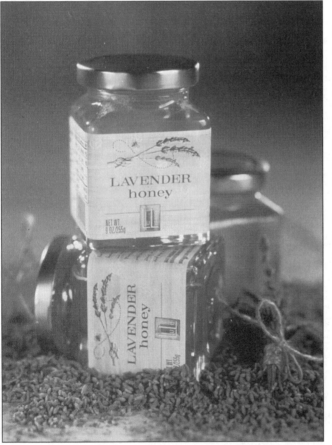

It will be unlikely for you to start out as the product leader in your category; therefore, you should think seriously about not being number two, but rather, becoming a market niche competitor. This is precisely why the specialty food industry works. Why is this? The leading seller of mustard, for example, may have a 30 percent share of the total mustard market, with a 10 percent net profit margin.

You, on the other hand, could carve out a 1 to 2 percent share of the mustard market, with a 20 percent net profit margin. The idea is to focus on overall profitability rather than beating the product leader in the market share race.

Market share is generally of little consequence to the entry level marketeer; however, you should know that major food processors seem to "allow" small companies about one percent share of a given market before launching a competitive campaign.

General Foods, for example, claimed a 38 percent share of the estimated $440 million specialty coffee market. If your new specialty coffee roasting business can sell up to $4 million per year, then you can expect some attention from General Foods. Otherwise, you will face most of your competition from other coffee roasters looking for a niche.

> **CASE IN POINT**
>
> *China Bowl Trading Company imported Chinese sauces, flavorings, spices and herbs. The company spent nearly 15 years in developing its share of the market before selling it to the Swiss-firm Estee, and later to Henry Ellis. The company markets to both the specialty and grocery food trades.*

Actually, if you can sell $4 million of roasted coffee, then you might want to consider a "buyout" by a larger company. It has been one way to make a lot of money.

Tapping Into Consumer Attitudes

Purchases of specialty foods have grown to more than $35 billion per year because of consumer demand for quality. Specialty foods represent affordable luxury. Even in recessions, purchases of many fancy foods tend to remain constant.

In the late 1970s, the United States experienced a consumer backlash to mediocrity. Notably, consumers had begun to take an interest in products with natural ingredients, no preservatives, and no artificial coloring. Purchases of fancy foods were based on considerations of quality and health.

The consumer backlash occasioned the remarkable growth of fine foods throughout the 1980s and 1990s. All of a sudden, everyone knew about brie. As more products were introduced, and new entrees proliferated, consumers developed a preference for a particular product brand or make. In the specialty food industry, the concept of brand preference was just becoming a factor in understanding consumer behavior. There is still plenty of room for experimentation, and, fortunately for new entrepreneurs, consumers appear disposed to continue in that vein.

With the exception of a handful of transition products, very few specialty food brand preferences have emerged. Those brands that are requested by name include: Heublein's Grey Poupon mustard, Celestial Seasonings herbal beverages, Godiva chocolates, and Häagen-Dazs ice cream.

CASE IN POINT

Almondina Biscuits—Started with $5,000 by a former conductor of the Ohio Symphony (who still guest conducts with a number of other symphonies) with his wife (a former member of the London Ballet). They were successful in five years and have been in business for 15 years. Sales are stable at the $2 million dollar level. Big help came from mention in Prevention *and* Women's Day *magazines. They use the Internet for direct sales to consumers and are getting more than 25 hits a day. Their Internet experience has been "like going from three cable channels to 700 channels."*

The specialty food retail business thrives on appealing to the senses. This makes for considerable impulse buying. Some of the most successful products are those sold in retail outlets where shopping can be an exciting adventure. There, new aromas and different tastes from sampled products surround consumers. Products with eye-catching displays and packaging further enhance this experience.

Once consumers become familiar with a specific product, they will then experiment with other products from the same line. For example, the Gourmet Line company's strawberry preserve will be tried. If it is liked, consumers will feel more disposed to try other types of preserves offered by the Gourmet Line company. Other producer's products will be tried only if unavailable under the preferred brand. If Gourmet Line does not have a blueberry preserve, then consumers may try one from another firm.

Finally, consumer attitudes toward specialty foods are influenced by that which is exclusive, new, and different. Products offering something unique will attract consumer interest. As long as these consumers want more new and better foods, there will be a continuing growth potential for new products.

Having said that, the growth of specialty foods in the 1980s occasioned a substantial widening of the traditional specialty food market to include greater distribution through down-market supermarket chains. When the recession of the early 1990s intensified, these supermarkets looked very closely at product turnover and began to eliminate some of the specialty food lines they carry.

In turn, the eliminated lines, once the bulwark of gourmet food outlets, attempted to regain their foothold in those outlets, causing even further fall-out in this widely over-assorted industry. Consider olive oil, which is presently over-distributed and carried in too many versions by too many supermarkets. The specialty food market, acting like a contracting accordion, has insufficient room to accommodate these and many other products currently in distribution.

Today, supermarkets are once again playing an important and growing role in specialty food merchandising.

> ## CASE IN POINT
>
> *A "bird's-eye" view of life in specialty food marketing: Condiments, mustard, tortilla chips, gourmet nuts, sauces, mixes, dressings, marinades, etc. Generally developed by persons with free time, lots of energy, creativity, and little money. Bankrolled by spouse and friends. Spend two to three years developing and packaging the product. Exhibit at trade shows usually in shared booths. Conduct demonstrations at retail stores. Lots of first-time sales, but few repeat orders. At third or fourth year, begin to realize this may not be their salvation. Then, they either take what they have learned, work up a business plan, and obtain financing, or go home and lick their wounds.*

Meeting the Competition

With whom will you compete? Aside from every other food producer, you will find your direct competition from others with similar products. Competition from other makers of condiments, for example, will occur when the consumer chooses their product instead of yours.

You will be competing for shelf space, too. There is a finite amount of shelving, and a growing number of products for the retailer to select. Fortunately, there is a lot of product movement. Product life cycles end, and products move to larger, down-market (grocery) distribution. As this occurs, specialty food stores demand products that will replace those that moved to supermarket shelves.

Consumer attitudes toward specialty foods are influenced by that which is exclusive, new, and different. You will be competing for the "scarce dollar." Consumers must want to spend more for your fancy sauce, instead of a less expensive grocery-grade catsup. Consumers have differing perceptions of different products. Many are impulsive—they like the packaging, for example. In fact, presentation of the product is often the sole determinant in the sale. Choices as to how to spend limited discretionary income are difficult to make. Products that impart the most "sizzle" will attract the most scarce dollars (see Figure 2.4).

In his book, *The Business Planning Guide* (available from Dearborn in English and Spanish), David Bangs considers the following questions in analyzing competition: Who are your five major competitors? How is their business—steady, increasing, or decreasing? How are their products similar and dissimilar to yours? What have you learned about their operation? How will your product be better than theirs?

FIGURE 2.4: "Sizzle" Considerations for Your Product

Packaging . . . . upscale

Labeling . . . . upscale, refined

Ingredients . . . . the best

Size . . . . appropriate (no giant or economy size)

Price . . . . on the high side (cost of production)

Shape . . . . upscale, but practical

High Volume versus Lower Volume-High Margin

A *margin* is the amount of money (profit) charged above the actual cost of the product. The specialty food trade consists of products that are characterized by low sales volumes and high profit margins. Profit percentages are higher in the specialty food industry than they are in the grocery industry.

The specialty food retailer will normally take a 40 to 50 percent profit margin; whereas, the grocery store/supermarket uses mark ups of 3 to 20 percent on most staple groceries. In some cases, supermarkets will use 20 to 40 percent profit margins for certain fast turnover items, such as bottled water, delicatessen products, and other products requiring service personnel.

The reasoning behind this difference in profits is twofold:

1. Industry tradition suggests that specialty food marketers determine their profits by computing them as a percentage of product sales, rather than adding a percentage to product cost.

2. Product turnover. Retailers need to achieve a targeted contribution (sales x margins) from space used. The specialty food retailer is likely to move ten jars of fancy preserves in a day. By comparison, the grocer may move several dozen jars of jam in the same period. Therefore, because it costs more to carry the fancy preserves, the specialty food retailer must sell the product at a higher profit margin. A

> ### CASE IN POINT
>
> Stonewall Kitchens, a Maine-based processor of jams, sauces, and other high-end specialty foods, is successful because of its quality products and beautiful packaging. A colleague who has watched the firm's growth reports that, "Stonewall Kitchens used to attend a local farmer's market where they would have a couple of tables loaded with the most beautiful looking products you have ever seen. They had unusual shaped bottles sealed with wax full of perfectly stacked dilly beans. What they were selling was rather ordinary when you think about it, but their presentation made it extraordinary. They also had numerous mustards, jams, and dips to taste and never minded if you stood there awhile tasting them all. They knew that eventually you would buy something. As their business has grown, it has lost some of that initial breathtaking packaging in order to fit on store shelves but they still try to keep their unique look."

further explanation of the difference between mark ups and margins will appear later in this chapter under the heading, "Pricing the Product."

◇ GUIDELINES FOR SUCCESS ◇

Product Development

(With thanks to Daniel Best, Technical Director, *Prepared Foods* magazine)

Network

Contact others in the supplier community. Also, contact independent labs, universities, and reputable freelance product developers.

Know your customer

Be "market-oriented" rather than "product-oriented." Region, ethnicity, and eating occasion can all affect perceptions of quality. Don't equate your taste preferences with those of your customers.

Identify product traits

Begin by defining all consumer-relevant product features in advance of development. Engineer the desirable attributes into the product (packaging, color, flavor, etc.), rather than defining product attributes after product design. Consumer test to determine how closely product variables match consumer needs and perception. Refine to reflect consumer reaction.

Manage your resources

You must manage by focus and flexibility. New products require time, labor, and capital. Investing in highly specialized processing systems closely married to a single product or product line is risky and expensive. Think long term. Apply processing systems that will be applicable beyond the immediate project requirements. However, by spreading your labor resources over a wide range of product development, you minimize the risk of generating both failures and superstars.

Guidelines for Success, continued

Maintain product quality

A long series of minute cost reductions will not reduce perceptions of quality in consumer testing. But, the end result will be compounded, and the overall quality of the product will suffer.

Control your costs

If your costs come in too high, then reexamine the basic factors. Are your ingredients priced too high, and are lower-cost sources available? Are alternative processing methods available? Can you find other market segments to capitalize on, and consequently increase volume projections? Was the projected price for the product too low?

Commit for the long term

Failure to commit can result in constantly changing signals and erratic funding. Focus on your strategic objectives and tenaciously commit to their long-term achievement. However, know when to cut your losses and pursue alternatives.

Pay heed to the time factor

Timing is critical. Too soon, and your product may not be ready. Too late, and someone else will be in the market with the same product.

Tactics and strategy

Do not mistake tactics for strategy. Excessive focus on tactics can leave you struggling for strategies to fit. Tactics are the processes employed to achieve your objectives. Your objectives are your marketing and financial goals. Strategies combine tactics to achieve objectives.

Manage by confrontation

Risk avoidance can become the path of least resistance when there is no freedom to fail. In your case, management by avoidance will stop you dead in your tracks. You simply cannot avoid making the complex and success-threatening decisions associated with specialty food marketing.

Producing Your Product

Because this is a marketing guide, little attempt is made to tell you how to produce your product. Your options are to produce it yourself—in an approved facility—or have it either co-packed or licensed to some other food production company.

We will devote some attention to product selection, packaging, and labeling, and invite you to contact the NASFT for their listing of companies that can package and help you produce your product. (See Appendix D.)

The food industry is notoriously "product-driven." You must make a clear connection between your product development efforts on the one hand, and the market and consumer demand on the other. Just because you are convinced that your new product will take over the market is no assurance of success. You must keep listening to your customers in order to exceed their expectations.

Contract Packaging

Co-packers are food processing companies that either have excess packing capacity, or are specifically devoted to packing other people's products. Their capabilities vary and some can only pack tinned (canned) products, while others can only package dry, non-perishable products.

You may want to seek assistance in formulating and packing your product. See the comments that follow and check with industry sources in your state, especially your state's business development agency, for assistance.

The complexities of moving a product from conception to market can be overwhelming even to experienced entrepreneurs. Developing network relationships with reliable co-packers will permit the small businessperson to achieve maximum utilization of physical and financial resources—and save time.

Working with co-packers allows the business owner to call the shots while drawing on various team members to perform, when needed, on a fee-for-service basis.

When you approach co-packers, be prepared to present your product and your needs clearly and concisely. You will be received best if you deal efficiently without wasting their time or yours. Be open in discussing your needs and their costs.

The major areas of co-packer operation include Basic Product Development Services, Food Processing Services, and Food Packaging Services. Each is described below (with thanks to John Darack, of the Dirigo Spice Corporation).

Basic product development services. These are often available from ingredient suppliers, such as seasoning manufacturers. Such service providers perform an important function by helping you convert at-home or menu recipes to a manufacturable form. Then, dry ingredients, and often several "wet" ones such as fresh vegetables, liquid sauces, condiments, meats, fats, and so forth, can be formulated into one specialized ingredient package. The resulting product can either be sold as an easy prep-as-is item, or sent to a processor to be converted into a canned or jarred finished product.

Using basic product development services accomplishes several of the following benefits:

✧ *Quality control.* The blender guarantees that agreed upon specifications for the product will be met.

✧ *Inventory control.* Only one item needs to be tracked, rather than several.

✧ *Recipe protection.* The blender signs a contract in which your recipe is kept confidential.

Finished product producers know only to add the simple liquids to a preweighed unit of ingredients.

◇ *Uniformity of finished product.* All ingredients are preweighed and batched. Opportunities for errors in production are eliminated.

◇ *Price stabilization and purchasing power.* The blender has the ability to purchase in large quantities from reliable and established sources. Cost averaging and unitized pricing eliminate being at the mercy of market fluctuations. You will know your costs over longer price periods.

◇ *Networking.* You will be "plugged in" to an existing array of related services, such as analytical laboratories, packagers, processors, marketers, and distributors that may not be otherwise available to the public.

Food processing services. After having your recipe converted into manufacturable form, you can bring your ingredient package and conversion recipe to a food processor. Be prepared to discuss the preparation of your finished product to your specifications. Liquid ingredients, process parameters, packaging, labeling, shelf-life testing, and possibly even distribution are topics you should address.

Be ready to deal with some practical limitations such as larger or smaller batch proportions, limited size or shaped containers, production scheduling, and ingredients availability (seasonally or otherwise).

Find the best fit—don't go to a large producer for small batch production. Conversely, be sure the processor has the capacity to accommodate your growth.

Food packaging services. If yours is a dry product, then find a packaging company that has the right equipment to make your ideal package. As with a processor, the right fit must be found. There are companies that specialize only in contract packaging.

Opportunities can also be found at plants that package products in similar-type materials to yours, and which would like to utilize downtime profitably. Good deals can be made here.

Co-Packer Benefits

Successful co-packing can provide you with the following significant benefits and cost savings.

- ✧ *Elimination of capital costs.* No plant to build or equipment to purchase.

- ✧ *Utilization of well-seasoned experts.* Solving problems that overwhelm you are a part of their daily routine.

- ✧ *Compliance.* Undergo the amazingly complex process of meeting federal, state, and local regulations.

- ✧ *Product uniformity.*

- ✧ *Purchasing power.*

- ✧ *Networking.*

- ✧ *Technical services.* (Often at cost or low cost.)

- ✧ *Marketing assistance.*

- ✧ *Distribution.*

> ### CASE IN POINT
>
> *Millicent's Preserves—Extensive line of award-winning preserves such as Champagne Pepper Jelly. Making jams since 1982 they have won many Los Angeles County Fair awards, including Best of L.A. award in 1999 for their Pumpkin Butter. The company has been in the specialty food marketing business for eight years. "Success is a combination of inner personal happiness and money."*
>
> *Vision: Turn company over to daughter in about five years.*
>
> *2000 update: Has Web site, won four more new blue ribbons, and may hold off turning over company for a few years until new grandchild is a bit older.*

A Word about Licensing

Many food entrepreneurs do not want to get actively involved in the production and marketing of their product. They think that since their idea alone has merit they can find a big food producer to whom they can license the formula and technology for their new product. Once again, this is an example of the product-oriented nature of the food industry. Very little attempt is made to find out what the customer needs.

There is very little to protect your formulation. If the big company sees your product as competitive, they will either copy (clone) it or make you an offer. Often times, such offers can be in the form of licensing or co-packing agreements. If you are fortunate enough to receive such an offer, then consult your attorney for advice about the nature of such contracts.

Food Safety and Sanitation Requirements

The U.S. Food, Drug, and Cosmetic Act is very specific as to sanitation requirements. You should ask the Food and Drug Administration to provide you with a copy of the Current Good Manufacturing Practice Regulations. These regulations set forth the requirements for establishing and maintaining sanitary conditions.

Food and Drug Administration regulations are contained in the Code of Federal Regulations. You can review these at a government printing office in your area, or from the Superintendent of Documents, Government Printing Office, Washington, DC 20402. There are nine volumes of Title 21, but only Chapters 1 though 3 will apply to you. They cover general regulations, color regulations, food standards, good manufacturing practices, and food additives, among other subjects.

In addition to federal regulations, each state has special requirements for inspecting and certifying food-producing facilities. If your initial production effort will occur in your own kitchen facility (separate from your home kitchen), then have it inspected and certified by your local food-regulating agency.

Product Liability

Many distributors will ask you to provide them with a current certificate of product liability insurance coverage. They will request that the certificate name them as an additional insured, to be included under "Broad Form Vendor's" coverage.

Be prepared to pay a hefty premium. Lately, when courts in the United States have found in favor of plaintiffs, they have awarded sums that have exceeded existing levels of defendant's liability coverage. As a result, coverage can be difficult to find and expensive to maintain.

✧ GUIDELINES FOR SUCCESS ✧

Government Regulations

Process	Responsible Agency
Business organization	State and local departments of economic affairs. Application depends on the type of organization (corporation, proprietorship, etc.) you elect.
Production	State Health Agencies. Sanitary certification, inspection laws.
Labeling	U.S. Food and Drug Administration. U.S. Customs (if you are marketing an imported product). Chapter 21 of U.S. Code of Federal Regulations includes the labeling laws.
Labor	Internal Revenue Service and state and local revenue agencies. Payment of FICA, withholding tax, and workers' compensation.
Tax	Internal Revenue Service and state and local revenue agencies for quarterly and annual income tax payments and procedures.
Distribution	Some states require registration of your products before they can be sold in that state. A well-known example of this is the Pennsylvania law requiring all baked products to be registered.

If you are setting up your own manufacturing facility, you will have to pay for workers' compensation insurance, as well as offer some sort of group medical insurance to your employees. Check with your insurance agent for guidance about the types of insurance coverage best suited for your operation.

Packaging Your Product

Packaging is the single most important element in the consumer's decision to purchase a new specialty food product. Packaging type and design are paramount to success in the specialty food trade. Attractive packaging is just one factor that prompts people to try new products. Other factors include:

✧ Coupons

✧ Price

✧ Reputation (the brand name is accepted widely)

✧ Convenience

✧ New

✧ Recipes included

✧ Influence of advertising

✧ Recyclable packaging

Ultimately, the purchasing decision is rarely based solely on packaging (except for gifts), but on a combination of the above factors.

Types of Packaging

The packaging you select will depend on the product. For example, different merchandising is required for bulk fancy foods, such as snacks and confections. However, if you have alternative packaging types to consider, then you should be aware of the impact some packages have over others. Witness the shape of the Perrier bottle. Packaging encompasses consumer perceptions, as well as practical considerations.

Glass containers are used because the product can be seen and there is no tin taste; whereas, canned (tinned) products are generally restricted to soups, pâtés, caviar, and most loose teas. Most consumers tend to prefer products in jars, rather than cans, despite a can's practicality. Also, cans are slowly being overtaken by a new technology called *aseptic packaging*. This type of packaging is widely used by fruit juice producers, but it can be used wherever a carton, plastic cup, or metal can might be required. These include fruit juices, coffee creamers, puddings, and yogurt. Aseptic packaging saves shelf space and is less expensive to transport because it weighs less than other types of packaging. You may find using this a challenge because of the equipment costs, but its use is growing, and the market for aseptic packaging has exceeded $2.5 billion.

Some of the fanciest packaging available is also the most expensive. At first, you will probably have minimum production runs, so you will not want to purchase thousands of empty jars, boxes, or other containers. The objective is to limit your initial costs, regardless of the economies of scale associated with large volume purchases.

There is little point in ordering a thousand jars and a thousand labels if you are not sure of selling a thousand units of your product.

Packaging types for specialty food products are many and varied. You can select from among readily obtainable containers made of cardboard,

CASE IN POINT

Truzzolino Food Products, long a mainstay of canned foods in Montana, retained the Chicago-based design firm Power Packaging to redesign its line of canned Mexican-style tamales (almost a cult food in certain parts of Montana), and its gourmet chile. The result was a very fancy-looking canned tamale. Despite making many of the right moves, the line never caught on nationally, and Truzzolino returned to its co-packing and regional food marketing activities.

CASE IN POINT

About working with co-packers, Boston-based Dirigo Spice Corporation Technical Director John Darack has this to say: "Being in business should be a rewarding experience. Don't fall into the trap of thinking you can do it all. Build and work with the team of experts who will remove the obstacles on your road to success."

plastic, wood, cellophane, glass, and metal. Try to find a good looking and reasonably priced container. Try not to pack your product in an odd-shaped container. As a rule, your product must be able to fit and stack on standard store shelves. It is wise to start with stock items (such as jars and lids) rather than design special molds, etc.

Competition's Packaging

It will serve your purpose to review products now on the shelves of specialty food stores. It stands to reason that, generally, you should package your product in a container type that is similar to those on the shelves. This comes under the heading of "you can't knock success."

It does not mean that your creative urges should be constrained, just that the consequent costs and requirements for educating consumers about your unique package may not be worth the expense.

Elements of Great Packaging

Aside from clearly conveying its contents, great packaging will cause your product to stand out from others. It will demand consumer attention and create interest in the product.

Visit several of your local gourmet food stores, and attend the next International Fancy Food and Confection Show to see examples of great packaging. The Fancy Food Show has a special display called Focused Exhibits. It offers you the opportunity to see hundreds of new products, gift products, and food service products away from the producer's show booth. And it will provide you with a terrific chance to compare differing packaging styles. Some products with great packaging are listed in Figure 2.5.

FIGURE 2.5: **Examples of Products with Great Packaging**

Category	Product(s)	Producer(s)
Condiment/sauce	Vermont Honey with Lemon	Herb Patch
Confection	Excellence Almond Creme	Kambly Meringue & Swiss Chocolate Cookies
Dressings/marinades	Various	Cafe Tequila and The Alder Market lines
Bagged snack	Seasoned Pretzels	East Shore Specialty Foods
Baked goods	Deep Dark Gingerbread Cake	Dancing Deer Baking Co.
Jam/preserve	California Harvest Fig & Lemon Conserve with Port	Grapevine Trading Co.
Entree	Chicken Breast Parisienne	Vivian's Home Gourmet
Packaged produce	Various	Epicurean Herbs
Sparkling water	Icelandia Water	Icelandia Water Corp.
Smoked fish	Gourmet Smoked Trout Fillets	Silver Creek Farms

Packaging for Warehouse Clubs

A growing market for specialty foods are the warehouse or club stores. Such chains include Costco, Sam's Club, and Pace. They like to have the product delivered from truck to the shelf location all in one step. They don't require slotting fees (see "Arranging the Deals" in Chapter 3). They do require, however, that you package your product either in large, nearly institutional, size, or that you bind your products together in a three or six-pack package.

Cost Saving Hints

Negotiate small initial production runs. Your unit costs might be higher, but you won't be saddled with thousands of a slow-moving inventory.

Limit initial production costs by using readily available stock items.

Packaging Considerations

In selecting the container and the means of packaging, review government regulations that may apply. For example, the state of California requires honey to be sold in 8-ounce and 16-ounce containers. Any other size is viewed as potentially misleading to consumers.

Most big cities have glass suppliers, and it is worthwhile to visit their showrooms, obtain their catalogs, and try your product in sample containers before making any final decision.

Increasing use of tamper-resistant seals suggests that you should consider employing such a device on your product's container. Also, if you want to add a consumer information neck tag to help educate the specialty food consumer about the benefits of your product, then this should be planned before you make your final packaging decision.

If you plan to sell to supermarkets, then consider such elements as supermarket shelf depth and height. If your product is packaged in a container that exceeds the shelf height, then it will be placed on the top shelf, out of direct eye contact. This applies to the number of facings that can be accommodated. If the product is too wide, then it will take up more than one facing per product. This may limit the amount of space that the store will authorize for your product or product line.

Outer Containers

The outer container is the shipping container. The most common outer container is a strong cardboard carton capable of holding one dozen units of your product. Because you will be making use of such pickup and delivery services as United Parcel Service, make certain that the outer container can withstand the rather substantial punishment shipments often encounter. A master pack capable of withstanding a 200-pound test, with a size of 18-inches square will fit nicely on a pallet, and make for easier and more cost-effective shipping.

Retailers are asking for products in smaller outer packages. Generally, one dozen products per outer package is sufficient; however, if you can break down the pack to two packs of six, you will find retailers more willing to try your product. Also, your suppliers can provide glass jars in 12-pack cartons that you can reuse once the jars have been filled. Often, these outer packs can be put into master cartons containing two-by-four by unit (one master carton with two inner cartons of 12 jars each), or four-by-six units (master carton with four inner cartons of six jars each).

> ### Size Points
>
> *Cost*: select best for your budget.
>
> *Selling price*: cost to consumer can influence container size selected.
>
> *Usage* (repeat sales): a 16-ounce jar may move once a month; whereas, an 8-ounce jar may move three or more times a week!
>
> *Shipping containers*: should hold no more than one dozen units.

✧ GUIDELINES FOR SUCCESS ✧

Packaging

✧ Describe packaging type used by your competition (jar, can, plastic container, etc.).

✧ Describe your anticipated product package type (should be similar type to competition).

✧ Is the proposed package a stock item, or does it require special order? (Check with suppliers.)

✧ Minimum order for stock item (supplier requirements).

✧ Minimum production run for special order (supplier requirements).

✧ Special handling required (e.g., cardboard to be lithographed or sticker labeled)?

✧ Special shipping containers required (box, glass, etc.)?

✧ Are co-packers available to package for you? (See Appendix D.)

✧ Does your package design conform to federal and local regulations? For example, honey in California cannot be put into 12-ounce jars; they need to be 8- or 16-ounce.

✧ Is your package size consistent with consumer demand? (Price will have an impact.)

✧ Does the outer container hold no more than one dozen (unofficial industry standard) of your product?

You may want to purchase mailing containers that can be used for individual direct sales and for shipping samples to prospective buyers. These can be sold to retailers when your product has a gift potential, allowing the consumer to have the retailer mail it to the gift recipient.

Other packaging considerations include the use of corrugated cartons, bubble wrap, filler materials, and associated equipment such as wrapping tape and tape guns. There are numerous sources for these, and almost any manufacturer or co-packer will be able to provide you with the name of a packing materials supplier.

Labeling Your Product

All labels must conform to government regulations. Even so, you will have a wide choice. Remember, your label is a crucial element in attracting consumers. It must convey the nature of your product, as well as the "sense" of affordable luxury.

At first, you should consider some type of pressure-sensitive adhesive label that can be designed and printed in small batches. Compare the costs of applying labels by hand and by machine. After you get the product up-and-running, you can have your labels printed in quantity. As with packaging, the color and style of your label will be important in attracting consumers.

Avoid the supermarket look with its reliance on bold lettering and lots of primary colors. The same company that packs your product will be able to help you have it labeled. Otherwise, you can hire labor to hand-label the product until your volume warrants automated labeling.

Uniform Product Code

This is an optic-readable symbol that can be affixed to your product label. The UPC symbol allows use of automated checkout machines and conforms more readily to other products on the shelves. As items are presented to the checker, they are passed over an optical scanner that decodes the UPC symbol and transmits this information to a computer. The computer stores price and other information on all items carried in the store. It transmits back to the check stand the item's price and description, which are then displayed to the customer and printed on the customer receipt.

The UPC code is an 11-digit, all numeric code that will identify the product. The code consists of a five-digit manufacturer identification number and a five-digit item code number. The 11th digit is a scanner-readable check digit. At this writing, all distributors do not require UPC codes; however, they are becoming more evident as food producers and distributors recognize the increasing influence the large grocery chains have in specialty food distribution. These chains tend to require UPC coding.

If you anticipate ever having your product on a supermarket shelf, it is less expensive and more efficient to have your initial label carry the UPC. In this manner, you will save labor by not having to affix it separately. Information regarding UPC allocation may be obtained from the Uniform Product Code Council. (See Appendix Q.)

The Nutritional Labeling and Education Act

Exceptions to the requirement for nutritional labeling include coffee, tea, and spice; containers too small to carry a nutritional label, and producers whose total annual revenues are less than $500,000. The Nutritional Labeling and Education Act (NLEA) of 1990 took effect in May 1994. A total work-up on a single sample to determine compliance with the NLEA by a food laboratory can cost more than $600.

FDA Labeling Requirements

Aside from your desire to impart ingredient information to the consumer, the U.S. Food and Drug Administration enforces label ingredient legislation. The laws require that ingredients be stated clearly, and in accordance with the regulation. A net weight statement is also required. In this connection, the American Technology Pre-eminence Act, that amends the Fair Packaging and Labeling Act, will require all packaging and labeling to use metric measurements of net quantity. The use of ounces and pounds would become optional. The law is very specific about the nutritional claims that can be made for any food product. Claims as to health, purity, low-sodium, and the like must be made in no uncertain terms. The code specifies what wording is permitted, and what wording is proscribed.

The FDA promulgated new labeling regulations in

1990 (Public Law 101-535) that require practically every food to have nutritional labeling. Regulations as to cholesterol content, and serving sizes are also being issued. Finally, there is some confusion as to which laws will take precedence when federal and state requirements differ. It will be necessary for you to check Chapter 21 of the Code of Federal Regulations, available from your local Government Printing Office, (or from the Superintendent of Documents, Government Printing Office, Washington, DC 20402) to determine the requirements as they pertain to your ingredient statements.

Nutrition Facts	
Serving Size: 2 Tbsp (36g)	
Servings Per Container: 14	
Amount Per Serving	
Calories 20	Calories from fat 0
	% Daily Value*
Total Fat 0g	**0 %**
Saturated Fat 0g	**0 %**
Cholesterol 0mg	**0 %**
Sodium 150mg	**6 %**
Total Carbohydrate 3g	**1 %**
Dietary less than 1g	**2 %**
Sugars 2g	
Protein 1g	
Vitamin A 6 % • Vitamin C 0 %	
Calcium 2 % • Iron 0 %	
* Percent Daily Values are based on a 2,000 calorie diet. Your daily values may be higher or lower depending on your calorie needs.	

There are regulations governing the physical aspects of labeling as well. Certain information has to be placed on certain parts of the label, and the lettering size has to be in specific relation to the overall size of the label, or "principal display panel."

What if you goof? The Food and Drug Administration will not officially approve your label; however, your local compliance branch will provide comment on the manner with which the label conforms to the regulations. If you sell the product with incorrect labeling, expect the FDA to enforce the law at the store level. It can cause all the product to be removed from the store shelves.

Labeling Considerations

One of your greater setbacks can occur when you recognize that your beautiful labels might be ruined by the label requirements. You must have a net weight statement placed in the lower third of the principal display panel, for example. If you know of this requirement beforehand, then you can save time and money by designing your original labels to allow for the legal statements. There are many ways of retaining your artistic appearance while complying with the law. Your labels should have eye appeal, be informative and legal. Remember that one of the key elements of a specialty food product is its presentation.

Labels offer more than practical and aesthetic forms of expression. They should be used to convey your sales message. Consider including usage instructions, cooking directions, recipe tips, and the like.

The front label (or principal display panel) is used for a different purpose than the side and rear labels. The front is the *tickler* that attracts consumer attention. The side and rear may include additional messages regarding the product use,

✦ GUIDELINES FOR SUCCESS ✦

Labeling the Product

✧ Will you do the labeling yourself?

✧ Can labeling be completed by a contract labeler?

✧ Can your initial label be produced in a limited quantity?

✧ Does your label conform to local and federal regulations (Code of Federal Regulations, Chapter 21)?

✧ Will your label contain a nutritional statement? Not required if total annual sales will be under $500,000.

✧ Is your label consistent with that of an upscale product? Does it impart a sense of high quality?

✧ Does your label stand out from your competition? Or, is it the same old, same old?

✧ Does your label give history of company, recipe tips, or other selling information?

✧ Describe how your label attracts consumer interest.

such as those mentioned above, or convey a message about other elements of your product. Remember the success of the "notes to consumers" on the cartons of Celestial Seasonings Herbal Tea?

Pricing Your Product

Earlier in this chapter I addressed the desirability of finding a market niche. Rather than concentrating on beating the product leader for market share, I suggested a goal of 1 to 2 percent market share with a 10 percent net profit margin. In striving for this goal, I underscored the use of margins instead of mark ups (cost plus profit). When using margins, profit is calculated on selling price. The specialty food industry uses margins instead of mark ups to develop prices. The following examples will illustrate the difference.

Mark Up

The unit cost of your peppercorn breadsticks is $1.00. If you were to use a 40 percent mark up, your selling price would be $1.40. To determine your selling price, multiply the $1.00 by $1.40.

$$\$1.00 \times \$1.40 = \$1.40$$

Margin

The unit cost of your peppercorn breadsticks is $1.00 and you decide to use a 40 percent gross profit margin. Your selling price will be $1.67. To determine your selling price, subtract .40 from 1.00 and divide the $1.00 cost by .60.

$$\$1.00 - \$.40 = \$.60$$

$$\$1.00 \div \$.60 = \$1.67$$

The different selling prices of $1.40 and $1.67 occur when you use a mark up versus a margin. The mark up is cost plus profit; whereas, the margin is calculated on selling price less profit.

Another example: Your honey mustard cost is $1.63. A 40 percent mark up = $2.28 selling price. A 40 percent margin = $2.72 selling price.

Cost Accounting

This involves computing all your costs, adding your profit, and the profit margins taken by distributors and retailers, to reach a consumer price (see Figure 2.6). No matter what the costs, if your price to the consumer is greater than that of the competition, you

---

FIGURE 2.6: **Selected Cost Factors**

Ingredients	Cost of Contents of Your Product
Packaging	Cost of outer package, the reinforced cardboard carton.
Production	Labor and materials used in getting the ingredients into the containers.
Containers	The jars, boxes, or cans used to hold your product.
Labeling	Design, artwork, electronic preparation, printing, and affixing costs.
Selling	Cost of making sales calls.
Promotion	Special events, trade shows, and in-store demonstrations.
Advertising	Sales literature, trade journals, and related media costs.
Administration	Cost of running your office, includes legal, accounting, etc.
Overhead	Regular costs of running the business that you will incur whether anything is produced or sold. Some include rent, utilities, upkeep, and taxes.
Draw	Your salary. Divide your annual gross salary requirements by 260 (average number of workdays per year) to get a realistic assessment of your daily pay. Divide that by eight for the hourly version. Even though you probably will not take a draw, knowing this amount will be helpful in your breakeven analysis.

will face substantial consumer resistance. It is for this reason that I recommend starting with your competitor's price, and working backward through the various profit margins to your product costs. Unless you have that one-in-a-million product for which the world has been waiting; in that case, demand will be considered "elastic" and you will have more leeway.

You may use either a cost-plus or market-set pricing method. The former begins from the bottom up, while the latter works backward from the consumer price to your product cost. My recommendation is to use the latter.

First, establish a consumer price (use your competitor's price as a reference). That will enable you to determine your gross profit after the retailer and distributor margins are deducted. Then, determine if your costs and profit margin yield a price significantly different from your competition. Applying a breakeven analysis that will help you determine the price range available for your product can assist some of your strategic thinking. A breakeven analysis will let you know at what point your dollar or unit sales will meet your total dollar or unit costs. Any revenue generated above the breakeven point is profit—below it is loss. Detailed discussions of breakeven analyses appear in almost all of the business management books on the market. David Bangs' *The Business Planning Guide* (available from Dearborn at 800-621-9621, extension 3650) contains a complete explanation of the topic.

Delivered Price versus Ex-Warehouse Cost

Depending on the circumstances, some transactions will require that you include freight charges in your pricing for a delivered price. Others will allow you to ship freight collect, or with the freight charges added to the invoice.

Ex-warehouse cost is the cost of the product (plus freight-in if you are importing) plus the cost of storage and handling. Your ex-warehouse cost plus profit margin yields your price to the retailer (see Figure 2.7). In these examples, we will use a gross profit margin of 40 percent, which is consistent with profit margins used by many food processors. In our examples, prices do not include freight, and they are called FOB (Freight On Board). The freight charge will be collect or added to your invoice to be paid by the buyer.

Your gross profit margin will include administration costs, and sales and marketing costs (broker commissions, promotion, reserve for bad debts, advertising, and the like). Your gross profit margin will have to cover all of these costs. You should aim for a net profit of at least 10 percent. (See the suggested pricing formulas that follow.)

FIGURE 2.7: **Pricing Flow Example**

Following is a pricing flow example from consumer price back through retailer, through the distributor, to your ex-warehouse cost.

Price to consumer		$6.25
Less 40%	x	60
Equals cost to retailer		$3.75
Price to retailer		$3.75
Less 25%	x	75
Equals cost to distributor		$2.81
Price to distributor		$2.81
Less 20%	x	80
Equals your ex-warehouse cost		$2.25

Customary broker commissions for sales direct to retailer = 10% ($.38 in the above example). For sales to a distributor the commission = 5% ($.14 in the above example). You will use the same price to the retailer, regardless of whether you sell to a distributor. Sales to retailers will entail less volume, but you will make more in profit (40% gross profit before broker commission).

Suggested Pricing Formula for Sales to Distributors

Formula: D = E ÷ (100% – P)

where,

D = Price to distributor

E = Ex-warehouse cost per unit

P = Gross profit margin

Example: E = $2.25 (product cost of $2.20 plus $0.05 for storage and handling)

P = 20%

Process: D = E ÷ (100% – 20%).

Then $2.25 ÷ 80% = $2.81 per unit. Your gross profit would be $0.56 ($2.81 less $2.25) for a 20% profit margin. Broker commission is 5% ($0.14) and will be deducted from the profit margin.

Most retailers in the specialty food industry work on at least a 40 percent margin. They will divide the cost to them from the distributor (or from you for a direct sale) by 60 to arrive at their price to the consumer.

Suggested Pricing Formula for Sales to Retailers

Formula: R = E ÷ (100% – P)

where,

R = Price to retailer

E = Ex-warehouse cost per unit

P = Gross profit margin

Example: E = $2.25 (product cost of $2.20 plus $0.05 for storage and handling)

P = 40%

Process: R = E ÷ (100% – 40%).

Then $2.25 ÷ 60% = $3.75 per unit. Your gross profit would be $1.50 ($3.75 less $2.25), for a 40% profit margin.

✧ GUIDELINES FOR SUCCESS ✧

Price Flow Worksheet

	Competitor's Product	Your Product
1. Price to consumer	$_____	_____
2. Less 40% (Retailer profit margin)	x 60%	x 60%
3. Equals cost to retailer	$_____	_____
4. Price to retailer (Same as 3)	$_____	_____
5. Less 25% (Distributor profit margin)	x 75%	x 75%
6. Equals cost to distributor	$_____	_____
7. Price to distributor (same as 6)	$_____	_____
8. Less 20% (Your profit margin)	x 80%	x 80%
9. Equals ex-warehouse cost	$_____	_____

Key question: How do the ex-warehouse costs compare?

This is before a broker commission of 10 percent. In this example, the price to the consumer will be $6.25.

Retailer price of $3.75 ÷ 60% = $6.25

You may find that the resulting consumer price of $6.25, in the example, is competitive for your eight-ounce jar of cooking sauce.

But, if you are selling a one-ounce packet of dill dip mix, then the product will be above the price point for its category, and you will probably encounter stiff consumer resistance.

Broker Commissions

Your gross profit margin should include, right from the beginning, the broker commission percentage. This will range from 5 to 15 percent, depending on the type of broker used. Brokers who sell to chain stores, independent wholesalers, and distributors will require a 5 percent commission. Sales via brokers to department stores, retailers, and gift shops will be commissioned at 10 percent. Brokers who have their own showrooms, and who call on retail gift and food stores, will require a 15 percent commission.

Distributor Margins

The distributor will add a profit margin to your distributor price, usually a minimum of 25 percent (divide the distributor cost by 75), to arrive at the distributor's price to the retailer.

Bear in mind the concept of price points, or thresholds, beyond which it would be imprudent to price your product. These price points are found usually just under the two, three, four, five, and up to ten dollar figures. If your price is $4.09, for example, you may want to consider lowering it to $3.99 or $3.95 in order to overcome buyer objections.

The margins and discounts in the above examples are representative of specialty food trade margins and discounts. There are many variations to these, depending on the product, market, season, and so forth. *You should prepare*

two separate price sheets, one for the retailer and one for the distributor.

Breakeven Analysis

Applying a breakeven analysis that will help you determine the price range available for your product can assist some of your strategic thinking. A breakeven analysis will let you know at what point your dollar or unit sales will meet your total dollar or unit costs. Any revenue generated above the breakeven point is profit—below it is loss.

Detailed discussions of breakeven analyses appear in almost all of the business management books on the market. David Bangs' *The Business Planning Guide* is the source of the following explanation on the topic:

The breakeven point can be calculated by the following formula:

$$S = FC + VC$$

where

S = Breakeven level of sales in dollars

FC = Fixed costs in dollars

VC = Variable costs in dollars

Fixed costs remain constant regardless of sales volume (at least until your sales volume grows so much as to require capital improvements, such as new buildings). They are the costs that must be met even if you make no sales. Fixed costs include overhead (rent, administrative, salaries, taxes, benefits), depreciation, amortization, and interest.

Variable costs are connected to sales volume. They include cost of goods sold (beginning inventory plus freight-in, warehousing, variable labor, broker commissions, etc. less ending inventory).

To calculate the breakeven point *in the absence of your total variable costs*, use the following variation:

S = FC/GM

where

GM = Gross margin (profit) expressed as a percentage of sales, and determined by adding gross sales to total costs (variable and fixed) and dividing the resulting total by gross sales.

Replace the dollar figures with unit figures if you want to determine the breakeven point in units produced instead of dollars earned.

Sample Breakeven Analysis

Total sales   = $216,000

Fixed costs   = $70,000

Gross margin = $57,680

Gross margin ÷ Total sales = GM%

Fixed costs   FC = $60,570

Gross margin   GM = ($57,680 ÷ $216,000) = 26.7%

Thus, breakeven sales = S = FC ÷ GM

= ($60,570 ÷ .267)

= $226,854 per year

On a monthly basis,   S = $18,905

If sales are projected at a total of $216,000 for the first year, you will not make a profit—but since you know what you are apt to face, you will be able to plan ahead to finance your business properly.

You can also use breakeven charts to measure progress towards annual profit goals. Suppose a $12,000 profit the first year. What sales would be needed?

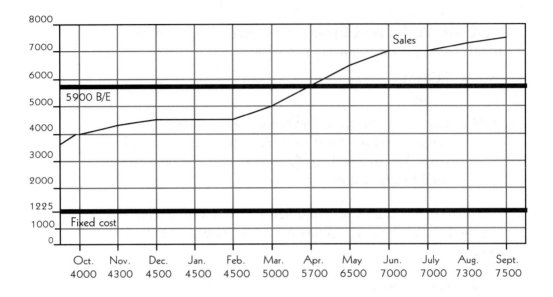

	Oct.	Nov.	Dec.	Jan.	Feb.	Mar.	Apr.	May	Jun.	July	Aug.	Sept.
	4000	4300	4500	4500	4500	5000	5700	6500	7000	7000	7300	7500

S = (FC + Profit) ÷ GM

      where Profit = \$12,000;

S = (\$60,570 + 12,000) ÷ .267 = \$271,797 per year
or \$22,650 per month.

Graphically:

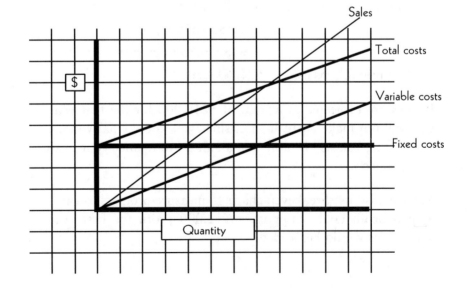

Anytime you can help your employees visualize progress towards a goal, you benefit. Breakeven charts are useful for more than financial planning purposes. Once you have calculated breakeven sales, you may find it very helpful to break the sales down in terms of customers needed. As a reality check, this can keep you from making overly optimistic projections.

Breakeven analysis may also be represented pictorially. The diagramming helps establish forecasts, budgets, and projections. Using a chart lets you substitute different combinations of numbers to obtain a rough estimate of their effect on your business.

A helpful technique is to make Worst Case, Best Case, and Most Probable Case Assumptions, chart them to see how soon they cover fixed costs, and then derive more accurate figures by applying the various formulas and kinds of thinking displayed below. This is of particular value if you are thinking of making a capital investment and want a quick picture of the relative merits of buying or leasing.

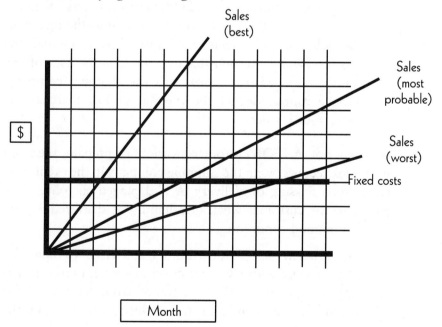

Understanding Terms

Terms are the arrangements for shipping and payment that you establish with your customer. Include your terms on your price lists. An important element of your statement of terms is the establishment of a clear credit policy, from which you should try not to deviate. Among the forms of such a policy are the following:

✧ *Terms of payment.* Either FOB your warehouse, or delivered, with entire invoice amount due in 30 days.

✧ *Early payment discount.* Offer either a 1 or 2 percent discount for payment made within ten days.

✧ *Line of credit.* Inquire of customer's credit references to determine just how much you should allow. Consider withholding shipment if there is an open invoice, or no more than two open invoices within the credit limit.

✧ *FOB (free on board).* FOB warehouse, or delivered, establishes who pays the freight, and when title passes to the customer. If your terms are FOB, your warehouse, then the customer pays the freight and takes title to the merchandise when it leaves your warehouse. This means that the customer will be responsible for taking up the issue of any damaged or missing cases with the shipping company. He/she cannot deduct the missing or lost merchandise from your invoice.

If your terms are FOB customer location, or prepaid, then you must seek recourse with the shipping company in the event merchandise is missing on delivery or is damaged en route. Title passes to the customer when merchandise is delivered, signed for, and in good condition.

✧ *Suggested terms.* To distributors and large volume purchasers start with COD (cash on delivery), until credit is approved, then 2%/10 days, Net 30 days, delivered. (This means that the purchaser may deduct 2 percent from the net invoice amount if paid in full within ten days. Otherwise, the total is due in 30 days.)

When selling to retailers use COD until credit is approved, then net 30 days, FOB warehouse.

Include the comment: "Prices subject to change without notice," on price lists and invoices.

Credit

Your ability to assess effectively your buyer's integrity will influence the procedures you undertake to evaluate "credit worthiness." Do not become overly impressed by buyers from high visibility/high prestige outlets. Rarely do these companies pay according to your terms.

> ### Invoicing Hints
>
> Do not print up thousands of invoice forms! In fact, with the use of a computer, you can generate a different invoice each time you make a sale. Use your invoices as sales tools. From time-to-time, add a special deal on your invoices to retailers. Many of the retail buyers are also the payers. Offer them a special "reorder deal" that they can send in with their payments, with the deal to be billed later.

The process. Request prospective buyers to provide you with three trade references and one bank reference. Ask for contact names and telephone numbers because some references will release this type of credit information over the telephone, and this will save time. You can expect that the credit checking procedure will take about three to four weeks, which is why I recommend shipping COD for the first order.

In the specialty food industry, most credit arrangements consist of the following:

✧ *Open account.* This means that you are satisfied with the credit worthiness of your customer, and that you ship on receipt of orders at your usual terms, wherein payment is due at the end of the 30-day period. Note that the specialty food industry tends to interpret payment terms of net 30 days, as starting on the day the merchandise is received, rather than on the date of the invoice, or ship date.

✧ *COD.* Cash on delivery is generally used with first-time customers, until their credit is approved. COD terms may also be used on request by some small retailers who prefer it to the requirements for accounts payable bookkeeping.

You request the trucking company to collect a specified amount, usually the FOB invoice amount, plus freight, plus any special COD charges. *Note*: This procedure will work only if you use specialized delivery services, such as U.S. Postal Service, United Parcel Service, Federal Express, etc.

✧ *Pro forma*. Used for prepayment. You prepare a standard invoice covering all of the costs agreed to (e.g.: product and freight) and type on the front of the invoice the word: pro forma. Send the pro forma invoice to your customer, and ship product on receipt of payment. Pro forma invoices are rarely used for domestic shipments (and then only in circumstances in which credit cannot be established or customer refuses COD). They are employed generally in those cases where buyer access to funds requires supporting papers, such as certificates of origin, etc.

✧ *Guarantees*. The only guarantee you will make will be against defects. If damage occurs during shipping, the buyer is usually called upon to pursue a claim with the freight company; however, it will be in your best interest to assist by offering to replace the damaged merchandise. Otherwise, some buyers will withhold payment of your invoice until the freight claim is resolved.

Warehousing and Shipping Your Product
Public Warehouses

These are companies that provide storage and warehouse services. Some offer cooled and refrigerated environments. They charge either flat rates by the month, or rates based on product stored, in-and-out charges, plus charges for preparing shipping documents (bills of lading), repacking damaged or broken products (coopering), and other related services. If you require public warehousing, then you should shop around to find the best combination of location, services, and costs.

Many warehouses will take your orders over the telephone and ship according to your instructions. This is where a facsimile (fax) machine can come in handy. Storage and warehousing will be an important factor in determining your ex-warehouse costs.

Common Carriers

Common carriers are trucking companies, other than the United Parcel Service (UPS) and Parcel Post, which offer pickup and delivery service. You will have to use common carriers for shipping large orders. UPS will take any size order, but no one container can weigh over 70 pounds (you can save money sometimes by delivering large orders in two or more shipments on UPS). Note that most common carrier charges are based on a minimum shipment rate of 500 pounds.

Your customer may request that you ship via a certain carrier. Most common carriers offer discount rates that are based on total shipment weight. UPS rates are based on the gross weight per case. Gross weight includes the product, outer carton, and shipping materials.

Rates are keyed to hundredweight, or per CWT (cost per hundred pounds). For example, if the quote is $4 CWT, then you will pay four cents per pound. Ask your warehouse to find the least expensive and most reliable carrier to fill your requirements.

If your production facility and warehouse are in your home, then you may have trouble working with a common carrier. They will be pleased to pickup and deliver your product, but you will have to arrange for the sometimes difficult process of working without a standard loading dock. Getting the product from your basement or kitchen, out the front door and onto the truck can be a trial.

Private Pickup and Delivery Services

The United Parcel Service is one of the largest and best known of the pickup and delivery services. Call your local UPS office and request an information kit. They will set up an account for you. They may require you to remit a deposit against which charges for shipping will be made. Generally, they charge a weekly fee for making daily calls at your pickup point. Shipments are charged by the pound, based on destination, and they offer redelivery, next day, second-day air, and COD services.

✧ GUIDELINES FOR SUCCESS ✧

Warehousing and Shipping

✧ *Establish warehouse arrangements*. Shop around for the best deal. A non-union warehouse offers greater leeway to remove samples, take inventory, etc., and is less expensive than union or "covered" warehouses.

✧ *Inbound*. Your product is shipped from your production facility, or pier, to the public warehouse.

✧ *Stocked*. It is inventoried and stocked in the warehouse.

✧ *Paperwork/records*. You will receive a monthly inventory statement and invoice for services provided, preparation of bills of lading (the shipping documents), storage, etc.

✧ *Select carrier*. You may request the warehouse to select a common carrier to ship your products to your customers. If you have frequent UPS shipments, you can also arrange for UPS to make daily calls on the warehouse to pickup and deliver the shipments to your customer.

✧ *Take inventory*. Once a quarter, or more frequently, you should personally supervise a physical inventory in the warehouse. This gives you a good inventory figure to use in preparing your accounts and in controlling your business, and it helps resolve any issues of missing or damaged merchandise.

✦ GUIDELINES FOR SUCCESS ✦

Warehouse Selection Flowchart

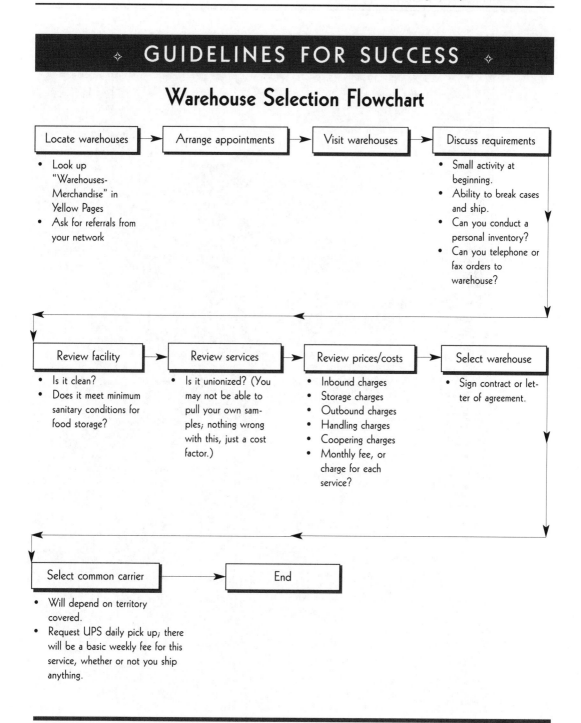

Locate warehouses → **Arrange appointments** → **Visit warehouses** → **Discuss requirements**

Locate warehouses:
- Look up "Warehouses-Merchandise" in Yellow Pages
- Ask for referrals from your network

Discuss requirements:
- Small activity at beginning.
- Ability to break cases and ship.
- Can you conduct a personal inventory?
- Can you telephone or fax orders to warehouse?

Review facility → **Review services** → **Review prices/costs** → **Select warehouse**

Review facility:
- Is it clean?
- Does it meet minimum sanitary conditions for food storage?

Review services:
- Is it unionized? (You may not be able to pull your own samples; nothing wrong with this, just a cost factor.)

Review prices/costs:
- Inbound charges
- Storage charges
- Outbound charges
- Handling charges
- Coopering charges
- Monthly fee, or charge for each service?

Select warehouse:
- Sign contract or letter of agreement.

Select common carrier → **End**

Select common carrier:
- Will depend on territory covered.
- Request UPS daily pick up; there will be a basic weekly fee for this service, whether or not you ship anything.

CHAPTER THREE

Taking Your Product to Market

This chapter offers a comprehensive review of the most fundamental aspect of specialty food marketing—taking your product to market. The chapter addresses the following elements:

✧ Six principles of marketing

✧ The role of the Internet

✧ Preparing sales literature

✧ Designing point-of-purchase materials

✧ Promoting the product

✧ Publicizing your product

✧ Advertising the product

✧ Finding buyers

✧ Establishing distribution channels

✧ Arranging the deals

✧ Appointing brokers

✧ Locating distributors

✧ Making the sale

You've come a long way in developing your product, and now you want to do a first-class job of placing it before the consumer. Remember to do the following:

✧ You continue to listen to your customers.

✧ You have developed partnerships with your suppliers.

✧ Your product is tried, tested, packaged, and priced.

✧ You have identified your niche and are ready to answer why you stayed with the enterprise: to promote, market, sell, and reap your rewards by exceeding your customers' expectations.

Six Principles for Marketing Success

Before you begin, you may want to review the following six principles of marketing that will underlie all your efforts:

1. *Focus.* Ground your business on the consumer, not the distributor or retailer. Know your market and be able to identify your consumer precisely. You will still have to meet the quality requirements of your distributors/retailers.

2. *Positioning.* Ensure that your product is not at a disadvantage to the competition. Differentiate sufficiently to clinch consumer acceptance. How does it stand out? What is its unique selling point?

3. *Demonstrations.* Demos sell. Provide tasting opportunities as often as possible.

4. *Advertising.* Center your advertising on the one specific advantage or edge your product has over the competition. Employ proven advertising methods.

5. *Distribution.* Establish distribution sufficient to the needs of the market. Make sure there is product in distribution to meet consumer demand, especially if you do any consumer advertising.

6. *Promotion.* Manage your promotions to increase in-store display to produce greater consumer sales.

The Role of the Internet

The global linkage offered by the Internet is driving everything in our economy. The rules of economic intercourse are changing. What effect will this have on specialty food distribution? Will there be a continuing role for the broker, or will these middlemen become redundant? How will you respond to issues of business-to-business services, marketer-retailer partnerships, fulfillment operations, cyber-shopping, direct marketing techniques, electronic customer challenges, new online food trends, Web page design, customer retention challenges, and developing key alliances? It may be time to review your long-term vision. What if your dream included the ability to market your products direct to consumers?

> ## A Note on Consumers and Customers
>
> Important Concept—Who is the primary determinant of quality? Is it the consumer? Or, is it the retailer/distributor? If your product does not appeal to the consumer, no amount of retail orders will ensure your success. So, if your product appeals to the consumer, then you must also know the quality needs of the customer—the retailer/distributor.

These are just some of the opportunities confronting specialty food marketers who wish to take advantage of the Internet. The following pages address some of the more important issues.

An Internet Home Page

You can create your own home page by using page-creating software provided by online services. You do not have to be technically adept, but it helps. A basic working knowledge of computers will suffice.

The real concern has to do with the effect your home page has on attracting customers. Since the cost of preparing a simple page is minimal—consisting of your time and talent and the access time charged by an online service—you might want to give it a try. Given the increasing level of Internet home page competition, a more sophisticated and complex Web page may be required. In this case, you would do well to retain the services of a professional Web page designer. (See Appendix I.)

Issues of privacy are being resolved—how to protect your customers' use of a credit card, for example—and more consumers are using the Net.

The Internet as a Means for Business-to-Business Services

Today there are over one billion Web sites! Among them are numerous pages devoted to selling specialty foods to consumers and to trade buyers (see Figure 3.1). The most promising, and most profitable Internet activity appears to involve what is called *business-to-business* (B2B) services. Imagine a specialty food buyer going to one Web site and searching among a vast array of product and pricing information, making a purchase, and then receiving one invoice. The B2B providers who capture this will be adding significant value to the specialty food marketing process.

> **CASE IN POINT**
>
> *Nearly 400 of the 1,600 exhibitors at the 1999 Summer Fancy Food Show have home pages on the World Wide Web.*

Think about getting together with your state's business development or specialty foods group. Use the Internet to set up a combined sourcing site for supplies. You and your fellow marketers could take advantage of the economies of scale such larger trading offers. A company called Inc2Inc is already doing this (not in connection with any state). Inc2Inc has created a digital marketplace that is capable of connecting trading partners in the food business. The site has been tested for procuring wholesale supplies for the baking operation of the Texas-based H-E-B grocery chain. H-E-B plans to use the site to purchase enormous quantities of flour and other ingredients used in its private-label bread, tortilla, and snack chips. Presumably, the resulting procurement efficiencies will lead to lower operational costs and to better consumer prices.

The Inc2Inc example will be out of reach to most specialty food marketers, but it does give one an idea of where Internet usage might head.

The Internet and Cybershopping

Home shopping via the Internet will dramatically increase in this century. Specialty food marketers increasingly sell their products straight to consumers via the Internet. This will affect new product introduction. The large companies, of course, can't do the same. Their size makes it difficult for them to adopt an adaptive and flexible approach to quickly changing market conditions. What they do, instead, is find ways to convince those cybershoppers to go to the supermarket via samples, coupons, and refunds for debuting products.

Cybershopping has a long way to go before bricks and mortar stores become obsolete. Tech-savvy consumers are becoming aware of such sites, but are wary that what might have been a private transaction at a local specialty food store is now part of a statistical abstract being developed by these companies. This is called user *profiling*, in which the site owner attempts to collect information about the buyer's interests, habits, frequency of use, etc. The resulting profile aids the supplier in matching its products and services with the perceived consumer's wants and needs.

Of all the factors influencing the specialty foods market, cyber-shopping has the most to gain and lose. As consumers become more comfortable with using the Internet to make purchases, there will be a greater likelihood that distribution patterns will change. Figure 3.1 gives you an idea of how many Web sites there are to shop at.

Issues to Address in Marketing Specialty Foods over the Internet

You may wish to consider the following issues associated with responding to the challenge and opportunity of online specialty food.

FIGURE 3.1: Number of Food-Related Web Sites in Spring 2000

Search Engine	Number of Specialty Food Sites	Number of Gourmet Food Sites
Lycos	77,872	94,079
Yahoo!	20	2,400
Infoseek	1,502	4,070
AltaVista	71,134	293,925
Web Crawler	38,577	110,957
Northern Light	498,826	251,016

Thousands of other sites are listed in the Excite and HotBot search engines. How does one get seen among so many? Select the Lycos search engine, for example. How realistic is it to expect that anyone would wade through 94,079 sites? Research reports that most viewers only look at the top 20 or so listings before either selecting one or leaving. There are a number of consulting organizations who develop Web pages and who have learned how to select words that give their clients top billing on these pages. (See Appendix I.)

✧ GUIDELINES FOR SUCCESS ✧

Sample Elements of Establishing a Web Site

✧ Server setup fee

✧ Service length in years

✧ Basic Web page design, type, and code

✧ Artwork of photo scanning

✧ Custom animations

✧ Image silhouetting

✧ Order form design

✧ Secure order form construction

✧ Internet domain name subscription shopping cart service via an Internet partner

✧ Page updates

✧ Shopping cart item coding (each item needs coding with identification, price, shipping, color, and size)

✧ Pagelettes (mini pages showing an enlarged view of one item)

✧ Cut charge (cutting a large group photo into small ones)

Mushroom Meringue Cookies, Chocolate Chix, Inc.

> Have you developed an Internet strategy to turn your Web site visitors into customers?

Strategic Planning

✧ Clarifying how Internet use can add value to your achieving your corporate long-range dream.

✧ Understanding and developing useful tools for measuring your Internet performance and comparing to your strategic goals and objectives.

✧ Understanding the implications of Internet security (both credit card and your computer).

Product Development

✧ Use the Internet to conduct consumer research, competitive research, and find packaging, labeling, and production services.

Marketing

✧ Understanding the impact Internet sales will have on the role of distributors, brokers, retailers.

✧ Establishing simple, yet effective, Internet relationships with retailers, brokers, and distributors.

✧ Branding your product name on the Internet.

✧ Using the Internet for market research. Determine specific customer needs, trends, etc.

Merchandising

✧ Effectively matching the right product with the right customer at the right time.

✧ Developing a community market where your products can be marketed along with complementary, non-competitive, products (called Multi-Store Architecture).

Customer Relations

✧ Developing effective means of cultivating prospects and turning them into repeat customers.

✧ Understanding the methods required for creating an outstanding customer experience.

✧ Providing frequently asked questions (FAQ) sections in your Web site.

Administration

✧ Developing easy and customer-friendly order entry and fulfillment processes.

There is the issue of consumer wariness to buy sight unseen. Some of us would be happy to refill our larders with a half dozen of that specialty mustard we like, but there are two problems with this. One is that the product is being offered to the consumer at the same, or even higher, price than offered by the nearby food store. An example: the 8-ounce crock of Kieller's Dundee Marmalade is sold at Trader Joe's for $3.28. The same product is available on the Internet for anywhere from $4.50 to $7.80! This is puzzling. The seller can take a longer profit than if it were sold to a distributor or retailer, and still offer a really good deal to the consumer. The other problem is that not many specialty food marketers are using the Internet to actually sell their products to consumers. They fear the negative reaction that might arise from distributor and retailers who would view direct sales to consumers as competitive.

A report by the University of Maine shows that nearly eight million consumers purchased *something* online during the 1998 holiday season. And this was expected to increase 400 percent in 1999. If this behavior continues, it will naturally include growing Internet purchases of specialty foods.

Most of the industry is viewing the Internet with some reservation. While some agree to sell to an Internet retailer, such as GreatFood.com, they

> ### A Consumer Vision
>
> You are the consumer. Using a hand-held scanner, you scan key ingredients in your cupboard, then download that information to your home computer. The computer conducts a search of all the appropriate Internet sites. Missing ingredients are added to your shopping list, and the food is delivered to your home.

may have to restrict use of the Internet to e-mail and reorders from their existing trade clients. Until the e-commerce marketplace has a greater impact on the bottom line, getting involved beyond setting up a Web site and an e-mail system should not be a high priority.

Preparing Sales Literature

Product sales literature is essential to your sales effort. A sales kit may consist of a price list, catalog (product presentation) sheet, product information sheet, and point-of-purchase material.

Typically, a catalog sheet and a price sheet will suffice. The catalog sheet is generally an 8½ x 11 four-color, product photograph accompanied by approximately 50 words of copy that describe the product. Include company name, address, and telephone and fax numbers.

In addition to price lists and catalog sheets, you may use a fact sheet to highlight promotable elements of your company and its products. Such elements as testimonials from famous people, historical anecdotes about your company, claims to fame, etc. can be included in the fact sheet.

Also, this is where you can amplify statements regarding recipes, applications, and health claims that relate to your product. These provide even more reinforcement of your sales message. Information that you include on your fact sheets may also be included on your price sheets. Lose no opportunity to impart your sales message!

Much of your sales materials can be prepared with the aid of your PC. There are several good software packages that are both easy to master and cost-effective. Ask your local software reseller for advice. The advantage of using your PC and a good laser printer allows you to work with and test a number of different promotional devices.

You can also prepare a leaflet or mailer on your computer that uses color. Complete the design using your desktop software and copy the resulting file to a disk. Take the disk to your local photocopy or stationery supplies store. You can have them print your color product using their PC and color printer. (Alternatively, you can buy your own ink jet color printer for under $300).

Effective Sales Literature Can Help

✧ improve distributor and broker knowledge of your product.

✧ convey preferred use.

✧ promote the product.

✧ make sales.

✧ GUIDELINES FOR SUCCESS ✧

Sales Literature

What to Include

Product description	Make it sizzle! Include the facts and figures (sizes, net contents, case lots, etc.) on the reverse of the catalog sheet. Use the front for the general presentation, and the back for the details.
Photography/graphics	Top notch, upscale.
Copy	Sell the product benefits.
Contact information	Company name, address, telephone number (don't forget area code), e-mail, and fax.

What Not to Include

✧ Prices

✧ Dates

✧ Any time-sensitive material (e.g., "just in time for Valentine's Day 1997")

Selecting Point-of-Purchase Materials

Many retailers find point-of-purchase materials (also referred to as POP) useful in attracting attention to products they stock. POPs not only attract consumer attention, they also inform and educate the prospective buyer about the product's benefits. POPs may include tent cards (used primarily in restaurants), posters, shelf talkers, product information neck tags attached to bottles and other packages, and recipe handouts.

✧ *Tent cards* are small, tent-shaped cards that can be placed on counters, tables, and shelves. You have seen these used in restaurants to promote specials of the day. Retailers use them to promote new products and to alert customers about items on sale.

✧ *Posters* are used in store windows, on store walls, and, when properly mounted, on shelves and counters. Because of their size, many retailers are hesitant to use posters, but they are especially useful during in-store promotions and in trade show exhibits.

✧ *Shelf talkers* are used extensively in the grocery trade. They are small signs that are designed to protrude from underneath the product they describe. They can be effective for new product introductions and are more likely to be utilized than posters. Also, they are placed under the product, rather than nearby, making a clear connection between the message they impart and the product they promote.

✧ *Product information tags* are most often used in the form of neck tags, which provide all kinds of promotional data. They may include recipes, company history, product uses, recommendations, ingredient descriptions, coupons, and free offers. The benefit is that you can ensure their use because they require no extra effort on the part of the retailer—they are already affixed to the product.

✧ GUIDELINES FOR SUCCESS ✧

Point-of-Purchase Materials

	Tent Cards	Posters	Shelf Talkers	Neck Tags
Size (approx)	5" x 7"	18" x 36"	6" x 10"	2¾" x 2½"
Color	2-color	4-color	2-color	2- or 4-color
Number to prepare	1,000	500	1,000	One run's worth
Distribution	Food service/retailers	Retailers	Distributors	With the product
When to use	Demos/special events	New products/ new retailers	New products/ new retailers	During intro stage/new products

Notes

Size: Tent cards are used on tables, so the size is small and the message brief. I have used posters with cardboard backing that can stand alone or be placed on a wall. In both cases, the posters were 9" x 14". Shelf talker size may be limited by the number of shelf facings available for your product. You don't want your shelf talker to use space occupied by another product. Neck tags are small and can be unfolded to reveal several pages of product information.

Color: Two-color products are recommended, where possible, to save money. (You can produce some four-color media on your own color printer or one available at your local copy shop.)

Number to prepare: Go slowly, prepare as few as economically feasible.

Distribution: Tent cards, posters, and shelf talkers can be shipped either with the product or via your broker and/or distributor. Neck tags may be used all the time.

Promoting the Product

One of the most important elements of niche marketing is product promotion. Product promotion often means the difference between success or failure. Getting your product before the consumer and having it recognized is the first step to making a sale. The most used means of promotion are trade show exhibitions, in-store demonstrations, giveaways, mailings, tie-ins, testimonials, show awards, and the Internet.

Trade Shows

Trade shows rate high on the list of important promotional vehicles. Other promotional vehicles are described later in this section.

Benefits of Food Show Participation

 ✧ Meet customers.

 ✧ Learn about competition.

 ✧ Experiment with product ingredients.

 ✧ Evaluate product packaging.

 ✧ Test product pricing.

 ✧ Rate various promotion techniques.

 ✧ Identify important trends.

 ✧ Solicit customer reaction.

 ✧ Make sales.

Food show participation offers a cost-effective means of introducing a new product, gathering market research, learning about competition, and making sales. There are numerous food shows, but few offer real value to most specialty food producers. See Appendix C for a listing of some of the prominent food shows.

The major shows held in the United States attract buyers from most specialty food markets. The level of exposure at these shows can be met or improved on only by undertaking the time and cost of traveling to many of the leading specialty food markets.

Certain trade shows require exhibitors to be members of the sponsoring association. Some associations require you to be in business for at least two years in order to be accepted as a member. If a member distributor or broker takes on your product, and thereby develops a client business relationship with you, then your products can be exhibited in that distributor's or broker's booth.

✦ GUIDELINES FOR SUCCESS ✦

Trade Show Milestones

One year before show

✦ Commit to attending the trade show.

✦ Begin work on total promotion campaign.

✦ Review booth design. Look for imaginative, inexpensive display schemes/materials.

Six months before show

✦ Make plane reservations and hotel accommodations.

✦ Develop sales literature for show.

Three months before show

✦ Check on sales literature produced by both your firm and the show sponsor.

✦ Review results in search for prospective brokers and distributors.

✦ Initiate contact and establish appointments with key prospects.

Two months before show

✦ Arrange shipment of any display equipment and samples (all display materials must be fire-proofed).

✦ Prepare press kits.

✦ Verify with freight forwarder that equipment has arrived. (Note: You can hand-carry samples/display materials from your car to the show booth. Generally, you cannot use any luggage carts or trolleys.)

✦ Confirm with show management that all arrangements have been made regarding shipping, electricity, extra tables/chairs, table drapes, signs, etc.

✦ Determine method for lead qualification following the show.

✦ Hand-carry a just-in-case package of samples, price sheets, and literature.

Upon arrival

✦ Set up booth display (table covers, samples, signs, etc.).

✦ Become familiar with show layout, transportation, special events, etc.

Guidelines for Success, continued

✧ Deliver your press kits to the show Press Room.

✧ Survey competitors' products, booths, product literature.

Upon returning home

✧ Write thank-you notes to the appropriate people.

✧ Record recommendations for successive shows.

✧ Begin business follow-up with potential customers.

Before attending a trade show, you will have to consider the appropriateness of your sales literature for the target market, including the illustration and currency of information. You will have to consider booth design, layout, signs, demo equipment requirements (you will have to order display risers, electricity, and floodlighting). A standard booth order generally includes tables, chairs, and booth carpeting.

The estimated current cost for a 100-square foot booth, with minimum spot lighting, drayage, table covers, freight in and out, travel, and accommodations and meals for one person is approximately $4,500.

As promotional tools, trade shows should be a part of a fully integrated and well-managed campaign. Trade shows should be incorporated into other promotional efforts for full effect.

Aside from the all-important trade shows, specialty food promotion can take many forms some of the most common are described in the next sections.

In-Store Demonstrations/Tastings

Consumers tend to buy products they have sampled, usually at sample tastings conducted at the point-of-purchase. These can involve a demonstrator, your product, and the means of sampling (crackers with cheese, for example). The demonstration is conducted during high traffic periods, over the course of three to six hours. Consumers have the opportunity to taste your product, to comment on it, to hear a pitch from the demonstrator, and to purchase. Often, demonstrations are accompanied by a special product price used to entice the consumer into making an immediate purchase.

A typical demonstration might be conducted from 10:00 AM to 3:00 PM on a Saturday. The idea is to get as much public attention as you can, so peak shopping hours are best for demonstrations.

Demonstrator costs will be in the neighborhood of $15 to $25 per hour, with a $100 to $125 minimum fee per day.

Giveaways

One of the least expensive forms of advertising and promotion is a product giveaway. A carefully managed program of free merchandise can place your product in front of the consumer, while attracting the attention of the retailer.

Usually, free merchandise is offered with in-store demonstrations, introductory deals, and sampling allowances. Free merchandise may also include specially packed sample containers for distribution at the point-of-purchase and during trade shows.

Mailings

A mailing can consist of a price list, a sample, and a catalog sheet sent to several retailers and/or distributors, or it can consist of a mass mailing with multiple inserts, full-color slick catalog sheets, and samples to thousands of prospective consumers. In entry-level niche marketing, mailings will be limited more than likely to selected retailers and distributors.

✧ GUIDELINES FOR SUCCESS ✧

How to Reduce Trade Show Expenses

✧ Share booth with another food producer.

✧ Share booth with broker/distributor.

✧ Take your own (flameproof) table drapes and riser covers. (Use a colorful oilcloth-type table cover for easy cleaning.)

✧ Use your own posters and signs.

✧ Order one double-neck floodlight per 100 square feet of exhibit space.

✧ Hand-carry your samples (no luggage carts with freight permitted through show doors, but you can carry boxes).

✧ Bring a hand-held vacuum to clean your carpet (touch up).

✧ Survival gear:

_____ Packaging tape/dispenser	_____ Fishing line (to hang posters)	
_____ Cellophane tape	_____ Paper napkins	_____ Marking pens
_____ Pliers	_____ Stapler/staples	_____ Ballpoint pens
_____ Clipboard	_____ Screwdriver	_____ Business cards

✧ Take a cooler (for samples, cold drinks, snacks, etc.).

✧ Use ice from outside exhibit hall for your cooler.

✧ Take hot plate (if required for sample tasting).

✧ Take serving materials (plastic plates, bowls, spoons, forks, etc.).

✧ Consider a less expensive hotel, and commute to the show.

It is very difficult for a new supplier to sell a new and unseen food product via the mail. Mailings should be made to prospective distributors in accordance with a complete marketing promotion. In other words, generate more than just a mailing! Devise a follow-up program that will include telephone screening and sales calls. A mailing should sell as well as inform.

Mailings to retailers are slightly different than mailings to distributors. Usually, they do not include the follow-up telephone call or the sales call. You will be mailing to many retailers, instead of a couple of dozen distributors, so you design a different mail campaign. The inserts you use should include a

✧ GUIDELINES FOR SUCCESS ✧

Mailings to Distributors

✧ Develop a mailing list. May be purchased through a mailing list broker. (See listing in Appendices.)

✧ Prepare the mailer and include a cover letter, catalog/price sheet, and a sample (if possible). The cover letter should be brief, informative, and to the point. Be sure to state that you will telephone the buyer next week.

✧ Prepare the envelope.

✧ Mail the materials.

✧ Follow-up by telephone in about seven days.

✧ Qualify the buyer (discern level of interest).

✧ Arrange an appointment.

✧ Send a brief note confirming appointment details, and stressing a benefit of your product.

✧ Call on the prospect, stress the benefits, and make the sale!

✧ Follow-up with a brief note about sale details.

postage-paid return order form for easy use by the retailer. Mailings to retailers are best used as: information providers, invitations to visit your trade show booth, invitations to request free samples, or more information and inducements to reorder.

Tie-Ins

You can get more out of your promotion dollar by sharing the costs with another food producer. This is accomplished by tying your product with another complementary product. For example, tea with pastries/cakes/cookies; cheese with crackers; preserves with special muffins/breads.

Arrange to have a series of in-store demonstrations conducted where both products are being served. Share the costs of the demonstration with the other producer. Presenting the two products in a special promotional package can support the tie-in concept.

Testimonials and Show Awards

One of the most effective, and least expensive, promotional tools is to get someone who is in the public eye to say something nice about your product.

Send your samples and product information to all of the important food editors in your major markets, as well as food-preparing personalities who appear on

CASE IN POINT

The following is an example of possible overkill in a mailing to retailers.

The following materials were received in an 8¾" by 6" envelope sent via bulk mail to retailers in January 1992 by a two-year old specialty food company that specializes in distinctive baked goods and confectionery:

✧ 2 empty cookie boxes, each with one-cookie capacity (0.75 oz).

✧ 1 deal sheet describing two deals.

✧ 1 empty cheesecake box (to hold one miniature 0.4 ounce cheesecake).

✧ 1 empty 1.5 ounce cookie box, to hold two cookies.

✧ 1 mailing list inquiry return card with special offer.

✧ 1 valuable coupon to save $10 off the regular price of a national retailer directory.

✧ 1 corporate logo private label offer and sample cookie box (for your logo, their cookie, and a cookie carton company's cookie carton).

✧ 1 six-page, four-color, 8½" x 11" brochure that includes a price list and order form.

Note: This is a very expensive, major mailing. Such direct mailings, in which "more is more" are atypical in the specialty food trade, simply because they cost so much to conduct.

radio and television. Include a press kit with press release, sample (if possible), company history/data, and a listing of where the product can be purchased. To assist you, if your budget permits, you may wish to have this accomplished by a professional public relations firm.

Submit your product to trade show management that has product award committees. Your product will be evaluated against many others, but if you win "best new product for such-and-such year," you can use this in your product literature, trade show exhibits, and advertisements. Both the testimonials and show awards offer third party endorsements that attest to the quality of your product.

Publicizing Your Product

A prominent public relations firm offers the following information about public relations.

Cost Effective

Public relations is a cost-effective way to draw attention to your product from a group of people who influence consumers. The targets of a public relations campaign are the editors and writers for newspaper and magazine food sections, and producers and hosts of radio and television shows that feature cooking and food products. A positive feature or mention in the press can be even better than advertising because it carries the implied, "seal of approval," of a respected source—the food journalist.

While consumer media reach the ultimate purchasers of food products, public relations can also be effective in expanding distribution by reaching retailers, brokers, and distributors through food industry publications.

Public relations should be a part of any total marketing plan, and, because of its relatively low cost, it can be especially important when marketing funds are scarce. In some cases, public relations can even replace advertising (see **Case in Point**).

Components of a Public Relations Campaign

There is no formula for a public relations campaign. It should be tailored to your needs, whether you are introducing a product in just one area or nationwide. The critical elements are an informative, well-written press release and an up-to-date, targeted mailing list. Depending on budget, include a photograph, tips on how to use the product, recipes, and a pre-written feature that ties your product to an emerging food trend. All of these elements, especially the photograph, can increase chances of pickup.

Many top editors want personally to try any product before writing about it; however, sending hundreds of samples can become prohibitive in terms of the postage alone. Consider sending samples to the top 100 prospects on your media list, return-addressed postcards requesting samples to the next 250 names, and a line on the release itself to call for a sample to the remaining names.

> **CASE IN POINT**
>
> *Nantucket Off-Shore Seasonings, a start-up operation manufacturing a unique line of blended herbs and spices, relied solely on public relations via trade show sales and telephone/mail-order to support its entry into the specialty food market. The news of the product's benefits (as told by their public relations firm) was one of the first of its kind and fit into current consumer desires for quality, taste, convenience, and low-fat cooking. The effort resulted in features in the New York Times, Family Circle, Food & Wine, Parade, and other publications. The favorable publicity convinced top retailers and catalog distributors that the product was worth carrying. This increased availability generated further publicity.*

Increase Your Visibility

While product announcements and endorsements can lead directly to sales, raising general visibility can be accomplished in other ways. A small ice cream company made the front page of a large metropolitan newspaper by handing out ice cream samples the night of April 15 to thousands of people waiting to mail their income taxes. A small company importing sparkling waters gained the same sort of name recognition by giving T-shirts to runners in a race. Other public relations vehicles include recipe contests and production of recipe newsletters.

If you are introducing a product nationally, consider retaining a small public relations agency that specializes in food products. Such an agency already will have researched and organized the mailing lists you will need and can advise on the most effective materials to use in your press package.

How to Know If a Press Release Is Successful

Knowing where and when a story has appeared is important for several reasons—first to know in which areas your potential customers are likely to have read about your product and secondly to see how the product is being received. This information can be used to fine-tune your sales messages.

Clipping services, such as Burrelle's and Luce, monitor newspapers, magazines, and radio and television programs nationally. They provide their clients with an original copy of each story that mentions the product name—or messages specified by the client—complete with the name of the publication, date the story appeared, and the circulation.

How to Write a Press Release

When writing your product announcement release, keep in mind the needs of the recipient. Food editors and writers want to know the "Five W's"—who, what, where, when, and why's—of your product so they can decide whether to pass the information along to their readers. You should also tell them about its advantages over competitive products and tips for using it, as well as any interesting facts about the development of the product.

The release can be printed on your letterhead. The general format should look something like the sample press release in Figure 3.2.

FIGURE 3.2: Sample Press Release

For Immediate Release:

Contact: (Your name and telephone number)   Date:

UNIQUE RUBS TURN EVERY BACKYARD CHEF INTO A GRILLING GURU

Now almost any food destined for the grill—not to mention the kitchen broiler or oven—can get "rubbed the right way." Rubs—uniquely blended dried seasonings that impart heavenly flavors to meat, poultry, fish, and vegetables—are destined to become the ticket to healthy, flavorful foods in the new century.

While grilling imparts its own heady flavor, the reason why grilled food seems to taste better when it comes from a restaurant kitchen is that the chef has usually treated it with herbs and spices to enliven the inherent taste of the food.

Now, these flavor blends—from green garden herbs and colorful peppers for fish to authentic Scotch Bonnet chilies and allspice berries for heady Caribbean flavors—are available to the home cook.

Nantucket Off-Shore Seasonings, Inc., has created a line of salt-free, all-natural, pre-blended herb and spice rubs to make everyone a grilling guru. The spectacular formulas are the work of Nigel Dyche, an island transplant who used Nantucket's quiet winter months to recreate the savory sensations of his summer memories.

Like fine caviar, the equally precious rubs are packed in handsome tins, since light is one of the primary reasons dried herbs and spices lose their color and potency. The terrific rubs come in six varieties:

FIGURE 3.2: continued

- Nantucket Rub: A blend of delicate herbs such as dill, tarragon, and fennel, flecked with whole pink peppercorns and given depth with garlic and onion. Whether rubbed on fishermen's favorites such as swordfish or tuna, on crustaceans like shrimp, or on the famed bay scallops from Nantucket's waters, the rub brings out all the best qualities of fish and shellfish. It makes a dynamite herbed chicken, and works equally well on whole pieces and boneless, skinless breasts. For a new twist, use Nantucket Rub to add zing to herbed garlic bread, as well as dips and salad dressings.

(Continue with description of other products in the line)

They are available at a suggested retail price of $_____ each at select specialty food stores nationally or by calling (insert contact telephone number).

# # #

✧ GUIDELINES FOR SUCCESS ✧

Public Relations

(as suggested by Brown & Whiting)

What Gets an Editor's Attention

✧ Write a headline that tells the story in two lines or less.

✧ Include all information: company and product name, product benefits, size and/or weight, kind of package, where and when available, and price.

✧ Include a photo if possible—5"x 7" black and white glossy and ideally a 35mm color slide. Be sure to identify the photos—they can get separated from the release.

Guidelines for Success, continued

✧ Provide a separate fact sheet so the editor can get the basic information at a glance.

✧ Be aware of publication deadlines. Newspaper food sections work weeks in advance, and magazines need three to four months lead time prior to their publication date. When in doubt, call and ask.

✧ Send the information to the right person. If necessary, call the general office number and ask who covers food and/or new products at the media outlet.

✧ Follow your release with a phone call to ask if you can answer any questions. But don't make a pest of yourself; leaving one message is sufficient.

Advertising Your Product

We tend to think that consumer advertising is the easy way to draw attention to our product. In the first place, your product has to be in the market before an advertisement directed at the consumer will work.

Occasionally, consumers will see inserts in the likes of *Gourmet, The New Yorker, Smithsonian,* and other magazines that advertise fancy foods. However, in the specialty food industry, the only advertisements that seem to be directed to consumers with any regularity in those magazines are ones that offer product via mail order instead of through retail stores. Successful consumer advertising requires ingenuity and deep pockets. According to the American Association of Advertising Agencies, the average American is exposed to approximately 7,000 advertising stimuli a day.

You are well advised to tread lightly when it comes to consumer advertising, especially if you are considering television or radio. Stick with advertising inserts in specialty food trade journals. See Appendix A for a listing of trade journals devoted to this industry.

Media Selection

Several of the trade journals will work with you to save money in preparing your advertisement. Consider retaining a small and hungry advertising agency. It will cost a little more, but the result will be better than cutting and pasting on your own. Make sure that advertising costs are figured into your overall budget in an amount equal to 10 to 15 percent of sales, or projected sales.

Some advertising can be accomplished using local radio and newspapers, but this is best done in connection with larger retailer promotions, such as those conducted by department stores.

What you undertake in the form of advertising will be determined by available funds. You will depend more on your own resources if you have a $1,000 budget and more on outside help if you have a $10,000 budget.

CASE IN POINT

Foods from the Wood—Company principal in business for six years with her husband. She feels she is successful because business is growing every year. They are on the Internet, but it is too early to measure the worth of this distribution medium. "Need about five years to determine its value."

Advertising Costs

✧ *Insert preparation* ($2,000 to $4,000). An insert is the actual advertisement you will have inserted in the magazine/newspaper. Many specialty food trade journals will take your computer-created artwork on a disk and produce it as an advertisement. You can expect to pay upwards of $4,000 for a black and white ad with about 50 words of copy. Illustrations and photography will cost extra. Traditional cost factors in a one-half page black and white insert such as artwork, copywriting, and typesetting can often be offset by creating your own with the aid of such software programs as Page Plus, Serife, and other desktop publishing software.

✧ *Photography* ($600 to $1,000). If you have a photograph made of your product, or product line, then arrange to use

✧ GUIDELINES FOR SUCCESS ✧

Advertising Hints

✧ Use the advertisement over the course of 12 months, or longer, and in a number of issues of different trade journals.

✧ Make certain the artwork and mechanical designed for the advertisement can be used in point-of-purchase posters and other promotional materials.

✧ Use the advertisement in combination with a well-planned and effectively managed advertising and promotion program.

✧ Coordinate advertising inserts with press releases, in-store promotions, show displays, mailings, and point-of-purchase posters.

✧ Don't waste money by running one fancy advertisement only once or twice in a single journal.

✧ Coordinate promotions with current and prospective retailer and distributor promotions.

the same photograph in your catalog sheets and other promotional materials.

✧ *Typical costs of insert space* ($2,000 to $3,300 and up). Media costs (the magazine or newspaper space) to insert a half page (vertical or horizontal) black and white ad will range from $1,400 to $2,000, depending on the magazine or newspaper. These costs can be discounted by running the ad more than once.

Finding Buyers

Now that you have had your product produced, packaged, and labeled, how do you find the specific buyers identified as a category during your initial market research? The type of customer you identify will depend on the type of product you have to sell.

Whether the product is canned, fresh, frozen, or refrigerated will influence its distribution possibilities.

Identifying the Potential Customer

We have numbered approximately 23,000 retailer prospects as potential buyers of your product. This figure presumes a product not requiring special handling and display, such as frozen and refrigerated foods. It presumes also an ability to get the product to all these prospects. About 15,000 of them will be able to stock refrigerated items such as cheese and fresh pâté. The competition for that space will be keen.

The number of retailer prospects swells substantially if your product can be sold in a gift store, of which there are approximately 71,000! Our 23,000 retailer figure includes only 10 percent of these as devoting any shelf space to specialty foods. More often than not, a gift store will carry a food product, notably candy, and will merchandise it as a gift, rather than food.

There are approximately five dozen distributors that specialize in selling specialty food to retailers.

In addition, full-line grocery distributors, of which there are hundreds, are carrying more specialty foods every year.

Qualifying Potential Buyers

Qualifying a buyer involves assessing the potential interest and likelihood of that buyer making a purchase. In the case of distributors, you do this by reviewing the product lines currently carried, mailing information, sending samples, and following up by telephone. Once you have qualified your buyer, you can then make arrangements to set an appointment for a sales call.

You can rely on your broker to qualify retailers, or you can make the call yourself to determine the interest level and to make the sale.

✧ GUIDELINES FOR SUCCESS ✧

Hints for Finding Buyers

✧ Exhibit in major (national and regional) specialty food trade shows.

✧ Arrange for one of the specialty food trade journals to conduct a mailing on your behalf.

✧ Contact the NASFT for information about their retailer and distributor members.

✧ Purchase a mailing list of gourmet food retailers from available business list consolidation services (Appendix Q).

✧ Contact Specialty Food Distributors and Manufacturers Association for member list (Appendix B).

✧ Contact National Food Brokers Association for member list; brokers can help you find buyers (see Appendix E).

Establishing Distribution Channels

You will employ various channels of distribution to get your product to the consumer. Understanding these distribution options will enable you to refine your marketing plans. In the specialty food trade, you will use either distributors (also called store-door distributors, full service distributors, jobbers, and wholesalers), retailers (including gourmet food stores, warehouse clubs, department stores and mass merchandisers), direct mail, and/or catalog houses.

The exact type of distribution used will depend on a number of factors, some of which include

✧ the market segments (e.g., product type or geographic region).

✧ the expected sales volume (large volume may require different distribution capabilities).

✧ the nature of the product promotion.

The profusion of specialty foods has made the process of obtaining distributor interest in carrying new products increasingly difficult. As a result, distribution often will require that you do all the pioneering yourself (selling direct to retailers) in order to attract the attention of a distributor. If you are lucky, your product may have sufficient appeal to attract a distributor as soon as you introduce it.

Before you approach a distributor, you should review certain aspects of the specialty foods business.

This list includes the topics you should know and which are contained in this book. Consult the table of contents or index for page numbers.

In order to successfully negotiate with potential distributors you need to be well-versed in the following areas:

◇ Pricing/deals

◇ Length of contract

◇ Post-sales support/training

◇ Performance measurements

◇ Territory

◇ Promotional activities—who pays

◇ How specialty foods get to the consumer

◇ The role of the distributor in this process

◇ Required profit margin/promotion support

◇ The relevance of introductory deals

◇ Details of your competition

◇ Specialty food pricing strategies

✧ Specialty food promotion strategies

✧ Marketing elements specific to the territory

Distributor Options Vary by Annual Sales Volume

Your distribution options will be more sophisticated at higher levels of gross revenues. Also, higher revenues will mean a greater commitment to funding advertising and promotion programs. The following describes the approximate distinctions between varying levels of sales and distribution schemes:

✧ *High volume sales* (+$1 million). The buyer has a warehouse, and is involved in mass merchandising where significant advertising dollars are required. Generally speaking this is not a major factor in specialty food distribution.

✧ *Medium volume sales* ($500,000 to $1 million). The product goes to supermarkets via rack jobbers (they do all the shelf work). Costs can include demonstrations and free merchandise. Some specialty food distributors have established relationships with both independent and major supermarket chains.

✧ *Low volume sales* (generally under $500,000). Products are delivered to a store's backdoor via wholesaler/distributor who uses brokers and own sales force or direct to store via your broker. This is the primary distribution option used in specialty food trade.

How Distribution Works

Distribution depends on the product, season, market segment, region, product stage of development, and consumer awareness/perception/attitudes. As mentioned in the introduction to this guide, as soon as you find a profitable way to distribute your product, someone else will be doing just as well with a similar

CASE IN POINT

Oualie, Inc.—A full line of Caribbean-style foods was developed in attractive packaging and with great promotional strategies. The owner/manager of the company was pictured on the cover of Inc. magazine. The MIT Private Enterprise Forum scrutinized her business plan. Yet, possibly because she did not want to "bootstrap" the product (literally putting it in the trunk of her car and making cold sales calls), she was unable to obtain financing. The business closed.

product, but with an entirely different distribution strategy. There are a number of distribution avenues open to you.

You can sell directly to the consumer by running your own retail operation, either in a permanent setting, or at special holiday fairs, for example. You can also do this via mail order. Send a mailing to prospective customers or take out a mail-order advertisement.

You can reach the consumer via a retailer, which will probably be your initial means of entering the specialty food industry. You put the samples in the trunk of your car and call on as many retailers as possible to make sales. Or make the sale and then ship to the customer via UPS.

Selling to a retailer through a broker is similar to the above, but instead of doing it yourself, a commissioned broker takes your samples to the retailers in his or her territory and makes the sales calls.

You may also reach your retail market through a distributor. The distributor buys your product and sells it to the retailer. Some products, especially heavy products in jars, generally require distribution in this manner. It tends to be too expensive to design the containers required to ship a dozen jars via UPS so they arrive undamaged at the retailer's door. (Nevertheless, direct to retailer sales are often necessary for the beginner, in order to create interest from the distributor.)

Sales are also made via a broker to a distributor to a retailer. Again, you employ a commissioned broker to take your samples and to make sales calls on distributors.

Your product may be sold via a catalog house, although very few catalogs have been successful selling retail packaged specialty foods. Those that are successful usually sell products that can be used as gifts. Some catalog companies will ask you to *drop ship*. This means that they send you the order and a mailing label, and you ship the individual product directly to the consumer. The catalog company pays you. You may also use a broker to make sales to a catalog house.

Significance of Exclusivity

All brokers and many distributors will ask for an exclusive territory. With brokers, the exclusive arrangement is to your advantage. It makes little sense to have two brokers competing for the same buyer with the same products.

Distributors often request exclusivity, especially when introducing a new product. It will make some sense to work closely with a distributor in a given market on an exclusive basis. This helps rationalize your marketing and distribution strategy. You might want to limit the arrangement, depending on the distributor and on the market, to six months.

Some strategies work for some producers and not for others. Many successful specialty food producers have never offered any exclusive arrangements. Once again, it depends on the timing, territory, product, price, etc. One way to ascertain distributor interest in an exclusive arrangement is to ask what sort of volume is guaranteed.

Food Service

A growing segment of the specialty food trade consists of selling to hotels, restaurants, and institutions offering better food service. Distribution in this market segment requires the use of brokers and distributors who sell to food service accounts. Food service opportunities exist for specialty food producers who supply fancy jams, preserves, and syrups and the like in single servings for use on hotel restaurant tables,

GUIDELINES FOR SUCCESS

Specialty Food Distribution Channels with Incremental Profit Margins/Commissions

*Commission paid from distributor's share of profit margin.

in room service and other situations, such as take out orders and picnic baskets.

Offering single-serving food products to food service outlets adds an opportunity to attain sampling and brand awareness because single-serving packages will be labeled with your brand name.

Providing your product for use as a prepared food ingredient will meet increasing demand by restaurants that are preparing more foods with specialty food ingredients. It is also a way to generate revenue during your start-up stage, and to reduce product costs by arranging for larger production runs. On the other hand, there is little branding opportunity for your products sold in institutional containers, and you will be subject to the vagaries of food service trends.

The food service sector is extremely price conscious. High-priced products are better served by creating demand first at retail, instead of wasting too much time exploring the food service segment.

The market is there, but you must be price competitive to crack it.

Mail Order

According to *Direct Marketing* magazine, there are more than 700 mail-order companies specializing in a wide range of food by mail, "each averaging about $1.5 million sales." As you may imagine, fruit, steaks, dairy, and alcoholic beverages account for most of the sales. Examples of these include: Harry & David, Swiss Colony, Figi's, Wisconsin Cheeseman, and 800 Spirits. The gourmet portion of mail-order sales comes mostly from companies that have retail operations.

> Recent data suggest that the specialty food and beverage purchases by mail order declined by 34 percent from 1998–1999. This decline has been influenced by the increased cost of postage, and by the growing use of the Internet.

Companies such as Zabar's, Balducci's, and Williams-Sonoma promote their products with seasonal catalogs.

Despite the decrease in purchases of specialty foods by mail order, a number of small specialty food companies have expanded their business and reached broader markets by the mails. Among these are Cost Plus, Williams-Sonoma, and Zabars. Notice that the latter are primarily retailers, and they use mail-order sales to increase business during holiday periods, and to offer repeat customers the opportunity of ordering by mail. The New York-based communications firm Ehrlich Creative Communications, Inc. provided the basis for the following advice to prospective mail-order companies:

> *Begin by testing your market. Select a publication you think your customers read. If they are well off and live in small towns, for example, try something like* Country Living; *if you plan to sell to a professional market (chefs or librarians), buy an ad in one of the trade publications, and so on.*

> *If you profit from the returns on the ad, then you may want to try it again. Advertising won't tell you much about the size of your market. If you get 100 responses to your ad, and 12 people eventually buy, is that good? The only way to know is through experience over time. You will be able to compare ad results from different publications, at different times of the year.*

> *You could try a co-op mailing. This involves using a catalog that advertises other catalogs, or using co-op mailings that include card packs and coupon mailings. The advantage of these types of mailings is that you get to compare your results with others in the program.*

Catalog Sales

Ask your catalog house to tell you its typical response rates. The catalog can't promise you a response rate, but it can give you a general indication of other companies' experiences. Determine what catalog fees include: creation of the ad or catalog cover? How many issues will include your offer? How many issues are mailed each year?

They can help you determine some aspects of the market for your product; however, it is not particularly scientific (you have very little control over who gets the mailing or whether they read it).

Another option is to get your products into someone else's catalog. This is one of the more cost-effective ways of getting into a new mail-order market. Your advantages include no up-front costs, no requirement for a full product line (you can run with just one product), a reasonably accurate idea of the demand for your product, and you may be able to get demographic and other information about the people who order your product.

Finally, you can conduct your own mailing. This is the most expensive option, but it is the most reliable. You will control all the variables—who receives your offer, when they receive, how it is presented, etc.—and you will get all the results. If you elect to go it on your own (produce your own catalog), then you will want to purchase a mailing list of at least 50,000 names.

The list is the most crucial part of your mailing. Test the list first, then your prices, offer, and copy. The rule of thumb for your test should be to generate 50 responses, or a return of one percent. This means a list of at least 5,000 names. You can get these lists from other catalog companies that serve markets similar to the one you want to enter.

You can count on spending about $15,000 for a 50,000-piece mailing, plus costs for producing the catalog or mailing piece.

CASE IN POINT

General Foods Corporation, with all its resources, was unable to make a success out of its much ballyhooed Thomas Garroway, Ltd. mail order specialty foods division. The company spent millions of dollars on full-page, four-color, advertising in major consumer magazines in an effort to sell gourmet foods by mail. I know of no successful gourmet-foods-by-mail enterprise in which a company ships a variety of different foods direct to consumers.

✧ GUIDELINES FOR SUCCESS ✧

Selling to Mail-Order Catalogs

(Adapted from an outline developed for the Roundtable for Women in Foodservice by Nina Dorsett, Director of Sales and Marketing, Plaza Sweets Bakery)

✧ The good news—mail-order buyers are accessible! Review catalogs and pursue those that seem a likely fit.

✧ Know your products well. Know their limitations. Understand what they will be put through. Do they require specialized shipping?

✧ Do you drop ship? What does this involve?

✧ Private label—yes or no?

✧ Properly price your product to cover all your costs and make a profit, yet allow enough room for the catalog to make its margin.

✧ Sales projections—how accurate are they? How do you plan?

✧ Be prepared to come through at all times.

✧ After the selling season, review catalog sales with the buyer. Try to get a commitment to continue with the product and take the opportunity to introduce new items.

✧ When exhibiting in shows, set aside a separate area to feature your mail-order products. Make sure your mail-order items are clearly identified.

✧ Remember catalog sales can mean volume orders and seem resistant to economic downturns. With more people having less time to shop, there is an increasing reliance on catalogs for gift giving and entertaining. The catalog market business is on the upswing and you should do your best to become a part of it.

Arranging the Deals

Because of the risks involved, both in terms of wasted time and expended resources, few of your potential customers will be willing to carry a new product automatically.

Consequently, most retailers, and particularly distributors, require special deals in order to earn extra profit during start-up and to introduce your product successfully.

The most common is the introductory deal. This can involve some combination of those described below.

With all deals, you can offer a "60 day buy-in" that allows the buyer to purchase up to a predetermined credit limit for 60 days and get the introductory deal.

Competition is so stiff in this industry that getting retailers and distributors to even try your product can be a major undertaking. The reasoning behind the deals is to help the buyer justify some of the costs and risks associated with introducing, or pioneering, the product. Most distributors, for example, would like to be assured of their normal profit at the outset of a product introduction, in the event the product does not succeed. In this way, they do not suffer a loss. They do not have to wait until the product takes off before they make a profit. The cost of deals is a cost to you, just as are ingredients, and must be budgeted and controlled accordingly.

Deals offer extra profits to the buyer, lower selling prices to attract customers, sources of funding for advertising/promotion and assistance in gaining attention over competing brands.

Note: Many of the following deals/allowances should be offered only if asked for by the buyer, and considered only if you feel the overall benefit is worth the expense. Weigh your decision carefully.

You will want to develop a long-term relationship with the buyer that may not evolve if at first you give the product away, and then later withdraw the deal.

The Overall Best Deal: Guaranteed Sales

As a rule, most food marketers only guarantee that their product is packed properly, and will replace any broken or damaged merchandise. Here's a thought: Think of how much you appreciate your local appliance/electronics store policy that allows you to return almost any product within 30 days of purchase for an exchange, credit, or full refund—no questions asked. Such a policy develops tremendous store loyalty. Wouldn't it be terrific if the food industry did that? What if you allowed your consumer to return the unused portion of your product for a full refund, no questions asked? If you did this, you could quickly carve out a niche that would appeal to almost any distributor or retailer. The offer would be for the consumer, only.

Of course, the matter is tricky in that we are dealing with a consumable. The CD player you bought can be returned, no questions asked, and then sold at clearance, thereby offering the seller an option to recoup at least the cost of the product. On the other hand, you are stuck with the half-used jar of mustard that was returned by an unhappy consumer.

Another twist of this would be to guarantee the sale, within a specific period, to both the distributor and the retailer. In other words, if your product failed to move, for whatever reason, either the distributor or the retailer could return it for a full refund or credit. In this case, it would be fair if the retailer or distributor who returns the product pays the return freight.

> ### CASE IN POINT
>
> *The Fancy Foods Gourmet Club <www.ffgc.com> sells gourmet food via the Internet. It offers a 100% Satisfaction Guarantee. The company will replace the product or issue a credit if the consumer notifies them within seven days of receipt. The guarantee, however, only covers spoilage, spillage, damage, or error. The company does not offer credits or exchanges if the product "does not appeal to your palate." Is this a 100% Satisfaction Guarantee?*

Free Merchandise

"One free case with ten, the 11th case is free." The distributors or retailers may use the free product in any way they wish. The retailers may choose to pass the savings along to the consumer, or the distributors may pass it along to the retailer, or either may take the difference to defer the cost of introducing the product and to increase profits.

Note that this differs from the offer "one free case in ten." Offering the 11th case free is preferred because you ship more product, which is, after all, the point. One free case with ten amounts to a 9.1% discount. Figure 3.3 shows the discount percentages with free merchandise.

If you specify that the free goods are for the retailer, then obtain proof of delivery for free merchandise shipped from the distributor to the retailer. In this way, you have greater assurance that your product gets to the customer, and you get the names and addresses of the customers.

FIGURE 3.3: Discount Percentages on Free Merchandise

Here are some other free merchandise discount percentages:

1 free with 2	=	33.3%
1 free with 3	=	25.0%
1 free with 5	=	16.7%
1 free with 12	=	7.7%
1 free with 20	=	4.7%
1 free with 25	=	3.8%

Sampling Allowance

Another free merchandise offer involves providing free product to the distributor (or retailer) so those free samples can be offered to consumers. This can also help the distributor get a retailer to purchase for the first time.

Demonstration Allowance

The demo allowance can combine free product along with a cash discount to cover the cost of a demonstrator. The demonstrator is retained either by you, the retailer, or the distributor, to serve and promote your product in the retail store. Ascertain beforehand the demonstrator's abilities, and the day and time for the intended demonstration. If possible, control and monitor the demonstration carefully, for experience shows that the absence of active producer involvement in control of demonstrations can waste time and money.

Prepare a standard demonstration kit that contains procedures you want to be followed in order for the demonstrator to be paid. It should include detailed instructions and an evaluation form that must be sent to you after the completed demonstration.

Demonstration costs vary, depending on the store and on the nature and length of the demonstration. Please refer to the section on promotion earlier in this chapter for a discussion of demonstration costs.

Special Terms

Many companies offer a discount for payment within ten days. This can be expressed as 2 percent, 10 days, net 30 days, FOB warehouse. This means that the distributor and retailer will pay the freight (either freight collect, or added to the invoice), and that their payment must be received by you on the 10th day, with a two percent discount, or in the full amount by the 30th day after delivery.

As an introductory deal, you can offer special terms to the distributor, such as: 2 percent, 30 days, delivered, which means that you pay the freight, and the buyer takes a deduction of 2 percent from the FOB invoice amount, which is due in 30 days.

You can offer any combination of these to either the distributor, or to the retailer. My recommendation is to stick to your original terms, unless it is a major purchase that would not work without special terms.

Freight Allowance

You can peg these to volume orders. For example, you might offer a 5 percent freight allowance for any order over 50 cases

of assorted product. This means that the buyer may deduct 5 percent of the FOB invoice amount from the payment. The idea is to encourage larger purchases by offering the benefit of economy to the buyer.

You can also calculate freight into your prices. Link these with three geographic zones—East, Central, and West—so that you will have three different, delivered, prices depending on customer location.

Your terms of FOB warehouse mean that the buyer is responsible for the freight costs from your loading dock to his or her warehouse or store. When selling to distributors, you may have occasion to ship freight collect. This means that the trucking companies will pick up and deliver your merchandise and will collect for the freight costs on delivery.

When shipping to a retailer, you may add the freight costs (usually United Parcel Service) to your invoice. Further discussion of shipping procedures and theory appears under "Warehousing and Shipping" earlier in this chapter.

Slotting Allowance

Many supermarket chains and specialty food distributors will require that you pay them a *slotting allowance* (also called push money and placement fees). This is a dollar amount that may be paid in the form of cash, cash discounts, or free merchandise, to cover the cost of slotting the product in the distributor's warehouse.

Ostensibly, the slotting allowance is exacted from the distributor by the supermarket chain in order to justify the costs, and risks, of taking on a new product. The result is that many new specialty food producers have had to seek other means of distribution, such as direct sales to small retailers, and thereby experience considerable difficulty in establishing full distribution.

Here's one way this works: your distributor will not even take your product to the selection committee unless you offer an appropriate slotting allowance.

You can expect that the distributor will deduct up to 10 percent of the gross value of your invoice. Often, distributors will deduct an amount equal to THEIR gross profit (your price plus their profit margin).

If you agree to a slotting fee, then you should demand proof from the distributor that the product has actually reached the store shelves. The requirement for slotting allowances is a hotly debated, and not a universally popular, phenomenon.

> ### CASE IN POINT
>
> *"Slotting allowances allow chains and distributors to make money on the buy versus the sell; therefore, success is being measured not by product performance, but by product profit. This has lead to virtually flat growth for supermarkets as opposed to nearly double digit growth within the specialty/gourmet food sector."*
>
> —Industry leader
> Richard Worth

Advertising and Catalog Allowances

Advertising allowances should be agreed to in advance, with specific elements of proof requested. Such proof of performance can include copies of the advertising inserts or circulars.

Another form of advertising allowance is cooperative advertising, wherein you and the buyer agree to share the cost of an advertisement in a local newspaper, or on a local radio station. You may be requested to provide copy, and black and white slicks (artwork on glossy stock) that depict your product and/or logo.

The use of advertising allowances (the buyer deducts the allowance from the invoice) and bill backs (you request the buyer to remit a bill to you at the end of the period) should be restricted to those opportunities that offer the best potential for sales.

Using catalog houses is a good way of promoting your product. In order to defray some of the cost of producing a catalog, an

✧ GUIDELINES FOR SUCCESS ✧

Deals in Review

✧ Free merchandise: A broadly employed, and cost-effective, means of getting new business.

✧ Sampling allowance: Similar to free merchandise.

✧ Demonstration allowance: A useful promotional tool. Requires effective management.

✧ Special terms: Not encouraged. Use only if in special circumstances (e.g., the buyer is planning a major promotion and requests extended payment period).

✧ Freight allowance: Used to encourage the larger order.

✧ Free freight: Use as special arrangement (trade shows, seasonal specials, etc.).

✧ Slotting allowance: Mostly required by supermarket chains and larger distributors. Try to avoid.

✧ Advertising allowance: Use for special promotions (e.g.: ethnic foods). Monitor carefully.

✧ Catalog allowance: For catalog sales.

---

allowance, usually 10 percent, is required by the catalog companies that will carry your product. This is a promotional cost to you because the catalogs generally carry your product only once, but you do get the residual benefit of putting your product before a large audience.

Appointing Brokers

Brokers are manufacturers' representatives. They do not buy your products. They take your product literature, samples, and pricing information, and make sales for you in a given territory.

Brokers receive a commission for sales made, based on your FOB invoice value. They generally receive 10 percent commission for sales to retailers, and 5 percent commission for sales to distributors. These arrangements, and commissions, can differ depending on the product and the market.

Brokers obtain supermarket authorizations and monitor distributor activity on behalf of the principal. Often referred to as food reps, food brokers also sell to individual retail accounts, small boutiques, specialty food shops, and gift shops. As food reps, they often maintain a showroom.

Note that most experienced brokers already have extensive lines to represent. On the one hand, a broker with several lines may not be able to devote much attention to your line, while, on the other hand, a new broker may not be able to make a living just selling your product alone. Nevertheless, the system works, and most brokers are interested in exploring new opportunities.

Brokers can exercise an important influence on developing sales for your products. They have access to buyers, knowledge of territories, and experience that you probably could not afford to replace in the form of a full-time sales staff. Brokers carry a number of lines, and they often provide the only cost effective way for you to get your product to stores in regions away from home base.

Because of this, there is a trade-off. Depending on the situation, you may have to take second place in a product line-up carried by a broker who is interested in your product. Unless the broker can see potential for high volume (read high commission income), then it will be unlikely for the broker to devote much attention to pioneering your product.

Brokers can help implement your promotion plans, including in-store demonstrations, and new product introductions. You will not require a broker if you can manage the territory yourself.

Locating Brokers

Broker listings are available from the National Association of Specialty Food Brokers (see Appendix E), and from advertisements in various specialty food industry journals (Appendix A). In addition, brokers regularly present themselves for consideration at the fancy food shows.

I do not recommend advertising for a broker in trade journals. It is more effective to ask other producers, retailers, and distributors for recommendations and leads, than to take a shotgun approach through an industry trade journal. Make certain the prospective broker understands your product, and knows how to sell it. You should meet with the broker to achieve a sense of how effectively you can do business together.

Broker Management Hints

✧ Visit the broker and make joint calls on key customers at least twice a year.

✧ Send monthly or bimonthly product information notes.

✧ Inform your broker of new products, testimonials, and all success stories.

✧ Work with the broker on planning your product promotions.

✧ Ask the brokers to visit and work your booths in the major trade shows.

Managing Brokers

Once you have selected a broker, you will prepare a contractual agreement (Appendix E) that stipulates the territory to be covered, conditions of sales, terms, commissions, payment procedures, etc. Remember, brokers work for you in specific, designated territories.

Send the broker a supply of samples, catalog sheets, price sheets, press kits, and other descriptive literature in the quantity requested by the broker.

To some extent, you may rely on your broker to provide information regarding the credit history of new accounts. You should also be able to rely on the broker to make a personal attempt to collect any overdue invoices. (Make sure the broker is amenable to this before you retain her/his services.)

Essentially, brokers are your representatives in the field. Treat them well, pay your commissions on time, and keep them

✧ GUIDELINES FOR SUCCESS ✧

Broker Evaluation

✧ *Years in business.* A well-established broker may not have room for your line.

✧ *Territories covered.* Is it adequate to your needs?

✧ *Major accounts called upon.* Do they include your prime targets?

✧ *Account requirements for deals, etc.* Can you accommodate these?

✧ *Lines currently represented.* Do any compete with yours?

✧ *Number of sales staff.* Sufficient to meet your needs?

✧ *References.* Contact three of them for comments.

✧ *Success stories.* Especially with lines similar to yours.

informed. You will attain a span of attention to your product directly proportional to the amount of time and effort you expend on maintaining the broker's interest. Make it easy for them to make money, and you too, will be rewarded.

Generally, brokers are paid monthly, or after the customer invoice has been paid. This is something you will negotiate when the broker is appointed.

Locating Distributors

Specialty food distributors (direct store distributors) buy your product for their own account and sell it to retailers, and to other distributors, using their own sales force and independent brokers.

As a rule, they offer the specialty food producer a higher volume and profit-generating alternative to direct retailer sales. The grocery food distribution system is very efficient. Because of this, it leaves little room for the lower volume specialty food product. Specialty food distributors fill this niche by carrying products that have not yet reached the level of consumption experienced by products in the grocery trade.

Many newer specialty food processors begin by selling direct to the retailer. A number of them retain this method of distributing their products even after they have gained a foothold in the market. With the increasing incidence of slotting allowances (see "Arranging the Deals," earlier in this chapter), most small companies will be unable to afford the cost of introducing a new product through distributors.

Distributors will let you know what they require. To attract their attention, you will most likely have to develop some of their territory first. This means selling direct to retailers. You will have to assess your circumstances carefully, and be prepared for the long haul, if you wish to continue selling direct to the retailer.

Distributor Services

Specialty food distributors offer a variety of services to the producer and to the retailer. Many, but not all, specialty food distributors perform the following services:

- ✧ Make sales calls on retailers and chain buyers.
- ✧ Purchase, inventory, and deliver your product to the retailer.
- ✧ Stock retailer shelves (usually only at chains).
- ✧ Oversee in-store demos.
- ✧ Prepare shelf diagrams for optimal display of the product (usually done only at chains).

✧ GUIDELINES FOR SUCCESS ✧

Appointing Distributors

Consider the following elements before you appoint a distributor:

✧ *Length of appointment.* Your letter of appointment should stipulate the period covered. Example: One year from signing, renewable annually thereafter.

✧ *Territory covered.* Stipulate which state, region, or large metropolitan area you are assigning to the distributor.

✧ *Promotional support.* Determine which combination of advertising allowances, special deals, free merchandise, etc. will be required by the distributor. Negotiate the details that are best suited to your mutual requirements and circumstances.

✧ *Frequency of contact.* You should attempt to be in regular contact with all your distributors. Use mail, telephone, and fax, plus personal visits and combined sales calls.

✧ *Termination provisions.* Your appointment letter should provide the means for terminating the contract. Either party with 30 or 60 days advance notice can effect this in writing.

Note: In many instances, you may have to take what is available and proceed without any formal appointment. If a distributor wants to buy your product, you cannot refuse on the basis of other distributor arrangements. This can be considered restraint of trade and is against the law; however, you can always appoint your distributor in a given territory as master distributor. That distributor would then sell to other distributors. In fact, once the distributor buys your product, you have no legal control over what he/she decides to do with it!

✧ Provide product sales and profit data to the retailer.

✧ Distribute point-of-purchase (POP) materials (obtained from you).

✧ Instruct store personnel in benefits of your product.

✧ Rotate shelf stock and remove unsalable merchandise (usually done only at chains).

Making the Sale

Now that you have an appointment, remember to take product samples, price lists, catalog sheets, pens, and a hand-held calculator. You will need the latter to verify your mental gymnastics. These will come about as you respond to fast questions about various discounts and quantity orders and other details from the buyer.

Use your price list as an order form. This will make it easier to process the order when you return to the office. Generally, you will not be required to give a copy of the order to the buyer. Many distributors will provide you with their own computer-generated order form.

Closing the Sale

The single greatest obstacle to closing a sale, aside from ignorance, is the fear of rejection! We all want friendly environments. We all want everybody to love our product, but we tend to avoid asking the most important question: "Can we write an order?" or "How many cases may I ship you?"

A great salesperson goes for the jugular! He or she never cries "uncle," no matter how many rejections, insults, or refusals received. The process is constantly being improved. No salesperson rests on laurels. All salespeople love selling. Learn about the importance of stressing benefits to the buyers instead of simply pointing out product features.

Listen to the buyer and learn how to handle objections (most of which can be turned to your advantage, once you know what to say).

Do not impugn your competition, especially if the company you are trying to sell to currently

Examples of What Not to Say
Buyer: "My color TV isn't working."
You: "I've had one sent to you from Macy's."
Buyer: "This stuff's too expensive!"
You: "Oh, here's $1,000 in cash to help you pay for it."

carries the competing product. This puts the buyer in an awkward position, for he/she probably made the decision to carry the other product, and putting the buyer's judgment in question may impede your further progress.

Your first goal has been achieved. You are in the company of a qualified buyer who has expressed an interest in hearing your pitch. Don't lose sight of your objective. It's not to make friends, or to have an informal chat. Your sole objective is to make that sale!

Keep in focus! So many of us go off on tangents. When you are stressing the benefits of purchasing your product, it is easy to react defensively when the buyer asks something like: "What am I going to do with just another _____?" The buyer is not tearing down your "baby." Instead, the buyer is looking for ammunition to help him/her make a favorable

✧ GUIDELINES FOR SUCCESS ✧

Handling Buyer Objections

Buyer: "I already have a dozen brands of mustard."

You: "Offering variety and choice is a specialty food trade strength. This is especially true in the mustard and condiment category."

Buyer: "Your competition offers a better deal."

You: "Let's compare the two deals, and I will consider meeting or bettering it."

Buyer: "Your product is just too expensive."

You: "Ours offers the highest quality of any product in its category. It is more than worth the money. Why not let your customers decide?"

Buyer: "I have no more room in my product assortment."

You: "You can purchase a smaller beginning order of the unique item(s) in my line." (For example, if your line consists of five different condiments, offer the one that is really different, not readily available from other suppliers, as the lead.)

Buyer: "Not now." (This is very common.)

You: "If not now, then when?" Or, "What would it take to make the offer of interest now?" (There may not be much you can do about this, except to offer to come back, call, or make contact by mail later.)

Buyer: (a retailer) "I don't want to deal with another supplier."

You: "I can ship COD, and save you the time and cost of setting up a new file/account."

Buyer: (a retailer) "I don't want to deal with another supplier."

You: "Can you give me the name of a distributor with whom you like dealing, and from whom you would consider buying my product?"

Buyer: (a distributor) "I don't want to do the pioneering your product requires in my territory."

You: (having made several successful sales calls in the distributor territory) "Here are a half dozen orders from retailers in your territory. All you have to do is deliver my product in your next shipment to them."

Buyer: (distributor who doubts worth of product) "We don't have any call for this product."

You: "People (retail customers) won't ask for products they know you don't have. Why not poll your retailer customers by phone or mail to determine the product's potential?"

Buyer: (who already buys similar products): "Why should I change suppliers and give you the business?"

You: "We're not asking you to abandon your current supplier—just let us supply you with a few items and let us prove our service and value to you."

Buyer: "Will you guarantee the product?"

You: "We will guarantee the product against defects and will replace or refund. We do not guarantee the sale of the product." (See earlier comments about guaranteed sales).

decision. Who else but you should know why it is important to purchase your product? Remember that you are providing a solution (benefit) to the buyer.

Sales ability is acquired. We do it in all walks of life. Make the call once you are solidly prepared, and practice beforehand. Don't let your pitch sound canned. It does not take a lifetime to master the successful sales pitch.

Specialty food buyers appear to want the deal. They are not interested, ostensibly, in product quality, variety, choice, or newness, per se. They want the product line that offers them the best deal—the one with the most up-front profit.

The buyer/seller dialogues on the previous page provide a small sampling of how you could respond to some of the more common objections.

Exporting—Sales in Nontraditional Markets

Food exporting can be both profitable and challenging. You will encounter requirements for pull dates in the European Economic Community, for example, and you will have to provide labels in a number of languages.

Nevertheless, always be on the look out for opportunities to sell your product overseas. For most specialty food products, this will mean sales opportunities generated by overseas visitors to your booth in U.S. trade shows.

This is especially the case with the shows sponsored by the NASFT and National Association of State Departments of Agriculture (NASDA). The latter organization focuses exclusively on promoting U.S.-made food products in overseas markets. The NASDA show is called "U.S. Food Export Showcase" and is held in concert with the Food Market Institute's Supermarket Industry Convention. (See Appendix C.)

Your first point of contact should be the staff of your home state's Department of Agriculture. They will direct you to the local resource for export assistance. In Massachusetts, for example, the Executive Office of Environmental Affairs' Department of Food and Agriculture coordinates export assistance.

At the national level, the U.S. Department of Agriculture's Foreign Agricultural Service (FAS) is the best source of information and assistance for entering overseas markets. Be advised, though, that the FAS has focused most of its energies on agricultural commodities. Only recently has the service begun to offer aid to what they call high value food products.

The FAS offers marketing assistance that includes trade leads, low-cost advertising in its weekly newsletter, buyer and supplier listings, and U.S. pavilions at major international trade shows.

In addition, foreign market information is published in government publications and research documents. Finally, the FAS provides market promotion, export enhancement, and credit guarantee programs.

A good point of contact is the Trade Assistance and Planning Office, USDA/FAS, 3101 Park Center Drive, Suite 1103, Alexandria, VA 22302. Telephone: 703-305-2772.

CHAPTER FOUR

Running Your Business

Many new food producers spend too much of their time marketing and not enough time focusing on the business and how to set it up. There are any number of ways to organize the structure of your business; you just need to take the time to define what works best for you.

Organizing Your Business

Your choices include a sole proprietorship, partnership, subchapter S corporation, limited-liability corporation, corporation, and other, somewhat complicated arrangements. Most of the companies in the specialty food trade are proprietorships. If you want to form a corporation, you can do so by calling a corporation forming service in Delaware. Costs run around $75; however, I would recommend that you seek counsel from a qualified attorney before you proceed.

Partnerships: What Are They All About?

If you are producing and marketing a product with a colleague, then you may want to form a partnership.

Benefits

Along with sharing profits, you also share the workload, expenses, liability, and taxpaying. Doing this takes a great deal of thought. If you are considering forming a partnership, you should find answers to several important questions:

Why do I need a partner? It may be as simple as needing additional money to invest in your business, or you might just want another person's expertise, experience, and industry contacts to help your business grow.

Each partner brings individual talents to the business. For example, one partner may bring sales and marketing skills, on the one hand, while the other brings design skills, development of new products, and warehouse management on the other.

Is the chemistry right? Partners have to be sure of compatibility. Each partner brings a different perspective. Similar guiding principles and moral philosophy will ensure respect for each other. Having the same philosophy is very important to a successful partnership.

> ### Focus
>
> Creating a business partnership takes work, especially since entrepreneurs tend to be very independent. People with such zeal find it difficult to fuse their efforts in one direction, which can be very costly.

One way to find out if the organizational fit is right before setting up the partnership is to set up a trial period. Avoid committing yourself financially until you are sure you and your partner(s) are compatible.

Can you trust your potential partner? A lot of your business activities will be based on trust. Business in the specialty food trade is done at arm's length. Partners who don't trust each other will suffer the consequences. Similar abilities and skill levels help, but understanding among the partners has to take place in an environment of trust.

> ### Consensus
>
> Consensus, according to the Saturn Automobile Company
>
> "70% comfortable, 100% committed."

Can partners be friends? Many a friendship has ended when friends live together or go into business together. Two or more people who get along as friends will not necessarily make good business partners. And, when you are friends before you are partners, it may be more difficult to offer opposing opinions for fear of hurting each other's feelings. Dissolving a partnership can be messier than the messiest divorce.

Successful partnerships are based on professionalism and attitude, as well as a burning desire to succeed. This doesn't mean you have to sacrifice your friendship to profit, it just means you have to base your decisions on business needs, not the friendship.

You must make a conscious decision, with each partner agreeing not to make business decisions unilaterally. This is where respect for each other's talents comes in.

Can you and your partners reach consensus? Partners must be able to compromise and reach consensus in decision-making. Once you are in agreement on your company vision, the direction you take will be clear to all concerned. Regular communication is essential to avoid the usual misunderstandings. Make time to talk about your business ideas only. Learn how to become an effective listener.

Financing the venture—who invests what? The amount of money you allot to the business can be determined by a clear understanding of who will be doing what. If the partnership work is not evenly distributed, will this mean a greater investment for one as opposed to the other? And, how will profits be distributed?

Will you need a formal agreement? Ultimately, no amount of paper will replace the basic trust and understanding between you and your partners, the kind of understanding that is sealed with a handshake. However, drawing up a formal agreement with the advice of a lawyer will clarify the issues and settle any future disputes should one of the partners decide to quit. All parties should write down all the issues each thinks is important. See where the issues converge and where they diverge. Negotiate the details. Reach consensus.

Figure 4.1 lists some of the elements your partnership agreement should contain. It is advisable to consult with a lawyer once you have worked out the various articles of your agreement.

FIGURE 4.1: Some Elements of a Partnership Agreement

✧ Date of agreement

✧ Names of all partners

✧ Business name

✧ Place of business

✧ Term of partnership

✧ Nature of the business

✧ Partner roles

✧ Finance and investment details

✧ Compensation details

✧ Who has authority to do what

✧ Termination provisions

✧ Special provisions

Processing Orders and Office Management

Many new food producers devote too much of their time and energy to producing the product. They think about marketing the product only after it is produced. But, once the orders are in hand, what then? Order processing and office management are employed in preparing the paperwork associated with shipping and paying for the order.

Accounts Receivable Bookkeeping

It will be important for you to understand some basic accounting. It is called double-entry bookkeeping, and it is easy to learn. Perhaps the easiest way is to purchase and use one of the many computer software applications specifically designed for this purpose. Among the better are Intuit's "Quickbooks" and ExecUtron Development Corporation's point of sales, inventory, and accounting software. A Certified Public Accountant (CPA) should be helpful in setting up a satisfactory business and finance computer software system.

Mr. Carl A. Lindblad, President of the Dedham, Massachusetts financial systems company Rubicon, Inc. (specializing in small business service), offers the following guidance:

> *From the very start, it is essential that you set up an accurate and informative bookkeeping system. An exhaustive study has revealed that of the eight primary causes of business failure, six are financial. They are: insufficient capital, inventory mismanagement, overspending on fixed assets, too liberal a credit policy, taking too much out of the business, and too rapid growth. The other two are lack of experience, and wrong location.*
>
> *Furthermore, it should go without saying that your business should have a bank account separate from your personal account. Personal funds should not be co-mingled with business funds, and all transactions*

should go through the bank account and not through distant cash or other accounts.

If you do not have a good working knowledge of book-keeping, you should hire the services of a competent professional to set up your books and teach you how best to use them. This applies even if you are unable to afford a bookkeeper or ongoing services in the early stages of your business.

In seeking professional help, check with friends and acquaintances to find a well-recommended accountant or bookkeeping professional. These may have designations all the way from CPA to public accountant to a bookkeeping service.

In your discussions with these firms, you will want to ascertain what sort of financial programs each offers. The more important systems include: income statements, balance sheets, the general ledger and budget statements. A brief description of each follows:

The income statement *is a historical report showing how your business did during a certain period. It is a primary source for business planning, and should contain such vital information as sales by product, cost by product, gross profit, expenses by type, and ratios used to monitor the financial health of the business.*

The balance sheet *is a snapshot of the financial condition of the business at the time stated. It not only shows the net worth or book value (assets minus liabilities) of your business, but also provides the remaining figures needed to calculate the important ratios of business analysis. Such ratios include liquidity, safety, profitability, and asset management. The ratios are important for financial control, and are used by bankers and other lenders when considering loans to the business. Your bookkeeping firm should be able to analyze the ratios of your business.*

The general ledger, *commonly called the books of the company, records all of the day-to-day financial trans-actions. The more detail, for later understanding, the better. Supporting the general ledger are subsidiary ledgers and records that may include: the employee ledger, sales journal, purchase journal, and inventory report.*

Budget statements *are estimates of future results. A carefully prepared budget will enable you to plan mar-keting strategy, production criteria, personnel needs, and financing requirements. A good budget not only supplies a reasoned road map for future operations but also yields essential information for potential lenders or investors. This is where you "plan your work then work your plan."*

The vital consideration in selecting a financial services professional is not the university degree or designation but the quality of training and the amount of experience such a person can bring to get your particular business headed in the right direction. Interview and compare the prices and experience of several such firms, and don't necessarily pick the cheapest one.

Your system should include a complete set of books, monthly financial statements, required tax returns (which do require a professional), and an accurate and aged tracking of accounts receivable and accounts payable transactions. Anything less puts your business at risk.

Essentially, accounts receivable bookkeeping is simply keeping track of who owes you money during a period in time. Usually, you will work on a monthly basis. I recommend that you employ a one-write system that reduces the chance of error, and saves time. With a one-write system, you use an accounts receivable control sheet and individual account ledger cards, along with a one-write binder. The control sheet allows you to keep track of sales and receivables during the month, and to allocate the funds involved using the columns provided.

You make entries when transactions occur: sales (or debits) and receipts (or credits). Each account ledger card is filed alphabetically by customer name, which offers you an easy way of keeping track of each customer account. Much of the accounts receivable bookkeeping can be accomplished with the use of computer software programs.

Dunning

Dunning is what you do when the account you thought was going to pay on time doesn't. If your terms are net 30 days, then around the 35th day, mail the first of three dunning letters/notes. See Appendix N for sample dunning letters.

About ten days after the final letter/telephone call, place the account into collection. There are a number of firms that provide this service. At the level of your activity, these firms will charge as much as 40 percent of the invoice amount to make the collection. If they fail, they will recommend that you seek legal recourse (as a rule, this is only practical when used for amounts over $5,000). This can be very costly, usually more than either the invoice amount, or the amount that may be awarded in court. Consider writing the outstanding amount off as a bad debt (a factor that should be considered in your pricing under a reserve for bad debts category).

Tax Considerations

Depending on the style of company you establish (proprietorship, partnership, corporation, subchapter S corporation), you may be required to file certain types of tax returns, both with the Internal Revenue Service (IRS) and with your state revenue service. The important thing to remember is to keep accurate and complete records of all your business income and expenditures. You will be well advised to seek the advice of an accountant when you first set up your books. The process of meeting your tax obligations will be less cumbersome if you get the paperwork in order from the start.

> **CASE IN POINT**
>
> *Pasta Fresca—1994 Outstanding Pasta: Jalapeno and Cheddar Ravioli with a Sweet Bell Pepper Shell. Also, 1999 Outstanding Pasta: Black Bean and Salsa Ravioli with Corn in a Jalapeno Shell. Well, these people didn't suffer from winning in 1994. In fact, they have grown to where their products are being carried in a number of Kroger stores, plus Giant, Hienens, and Food Emporium. The company has a complete line of easy-to-prepare, upscale flavored, easy-to-eat pasta with fresh, natural ingredients.*

Forms Usage and Filing

Many of your basic supplies including invoices, envelopes, price sheets, letterhead stationery, address labels, credit check forms, and dunning letter/forms can be designed with the help of a personal computer. Use a rubber stamp if you do not want to have 1,000 copies of something printed.

Your computer can generate invoices. Forget about running your business without a personal computer. I know this sounds dramatic, but the 21st century is upon us and no business can be the least professional—or profitable—without the application of computers. Figure 4.2 suggests some tips to get maximum mileage out of your invoice.

FIGURE 4.2: Tips to Get Maximum Mileage Out of Invoices

The invoice parts may be used for some or all of the following purposes:

Part 1. Customer via mail

Part 2. Broker via e-mail

Part 3. Accounts receivable (no need to produce a hard copy; use your electronic file)

Part 4. Shipping confirmation via e-mail

Part 5. Warehouse copy via e-mail

Part 6. Packing slip via e-mail

See Appendix N for sample forms.

Naturally, you will want to maintain files of all your business correspondence, accounts receivable, accounts payable, completed sales transactions, etc. Generally, files are kept current for one year, then placed in a different drawer. Keep one current year file drawer, plus files for the past two years. Files from earlier years may be retired to boxes and should be stored for at least seven years (for tax purposes).

Filing should be set up in accordance with what makes life easier for you. Files should have some rationale that is easy to remember and easy to employ. A file set up for completed sales transactions alphabetically by geographic location is one of the easiest to use. The actual filing of paper will not be necessary for most of the aforementioned since the same thing can be achieved with your computer and accounting software.

Notwithstanding my statement about computer importance, we still need some paper backup for our records. Make certain to back up your computer files—in fact, you may want to "zip" them up instead. There are a number of software titles that can do this. I recommend PKWare's PKZIP.EXE, for example, or use a special ZIP drive and disk. This saves the whole file, and you do not have to confront the troubles I have sometimes experienced with backed up files.

Order Processing Flow

For the computer user (you), there are a number of good software packages that you can employ to keep track of your transactions. Software such as Quicken, CashGraf, and One-Write Plus Accounting to name a few, offer full business accounting systems. Until you get the requisite software, you will need the following order processing supplies. A "one-write" accounting system, consisting of binder, journal forms, and ledger cards. The accompanying flowchart shown on the following pages can be applied to understanding and clarifying both manual and computer applications.

Notes to Order Processing Flow

The flow shows both hard copy and software order processing. You will not have to place invoice copies in a hold file if you are using a software-generated invoice.] Simply file the information in the customer's computer account. No need for hardcopies beyond those mailed to the customer.

GUIDELINES FOR SUCCESS

Order Processing Flowchart

(Some of the processes will not be required if you use order processing software)

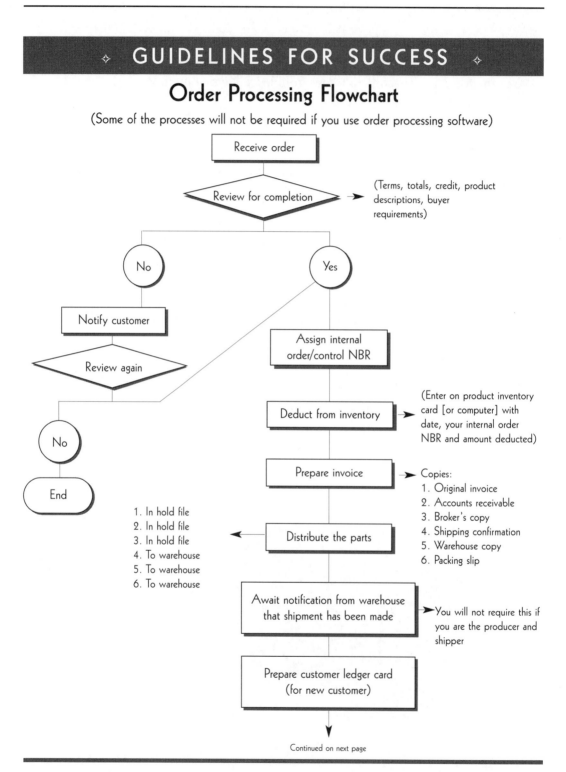

Receive order

Review for completion → (Terms, totals, credit, product descriptions, buyer requirements)

No / Yes

Notify customer

Review again

No

End

Assign internal order/control NBR

Deduct from inventory → (Enter on product inventory card [or computer] with date, your internal order NBR and amount deducted)

Prepare invoice → Copies:
1. Original invoice
2. Accounts receivable
3. Broker's copy
4. Shipping confirmation
5. Warehouse copy
6. Packing slip

1. In hold file
2. In hold file
3. In hold file
4. To warehouse
5. To warehouse
6. To warehouse

Distribute the parts

Await notification from warehouse that shipment has been made → You will not require this if you are the producer and shipper

Prepare customer ledger card (for new customer)

Continued on next page

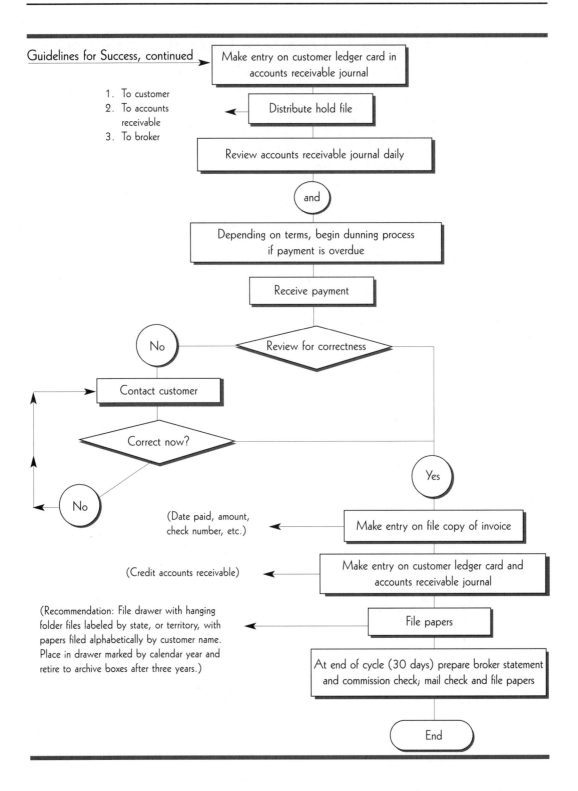

Guidelines for Success, continued

1. To customer
2. To accounts receivable
3. To broker

Make entry on customer ledger card in accounts receivable journal

Distribute hold file

Review accounts receivable journal daily

and

Depending on terms, begin dunning process if payment is overdue

Receive payment

Review for correctness

No

Contact customer

Correct now?

No

Yes

Make entry on file copy of invoice

(Date paid, amount, check number, etc.)

Make entry on customer ledger card and accounts receivable journal

(Credit accounts receivable)

File papers

(Recommendation: File drawer with hanging folder files labeled by state, or territory, with papers filed alphabetically by customer name. Place in drawer marked by calendar year and retire to archive boxes after three years.)

At end of cycle (30 days) prepare broker statement and commission check; mail check and file papers

End

Developing Long-Term Customer Relationships

The basic theory of good customer service is to operate for the convenience of your customer. This means that you call the customer back instead of asking the customer to return your call. You accept the responsibility for getting answers to customers' questions. Don't ask them to telephone someone else to get an answer. The examples are endless. Suffice it to say that many food producers fail to get the point about customer service: it is service to the customer.

Customer Feedback Hint

Include a customer satisfaction card in your shipment or with your invoice to retailers. This can be a form that allows the customer to comment on the condition of the product or the nature of any of your services. It can also be designed as a convenient and easy-to-use reorder form. Consider having it postage paid.

One often overlooked aspect of marketing is the follow-up process after the order is shipped. Sometimes this is simply a telephone call or visit to see that all arrived in good order. This helps cement your professional relationship and it creates goodwill. You impress the customer as someone who will stay around, and not run off with the check.

Consider telephone marketing to ensure that customer contact is maintained. In those areas where you are not using a broker, you can generate continued sales over the telephone. You can use the telephone and the mails to contact all your customers, regardless of broker use, regarding special promotions. Alert your broker of any subsequent interest so that a sales call can be made.

Earlier, we talked about the distinction between customer and consumer. The consumer consumes your product, the customer buys it for resale. The latter determines the quality of your service/product. Your success can be measured only on how you meet your customers' quality needs.

PURELY AMERICAN

GREAT FINDS IN REGIONAL AMERICAN FOODS   ®

CHAPTER FIVE

Creating Your Own Success Niche

We began this book by testing your motivation. You learned that obtaining nationwide distribution—in every grocery on every corner in every city and town—costs the market leaders a fortune. There are more than 15,000 new food products introduced every year, and there is a 96 percent failure rate over the first three years. Yet, here you are, now versed in the methods and procedures for marketing your specialty food product. Or, armed as you are with the knowledge, you have decided, or are about to decide, that it just is not for you. Perhaps, you are going to give it a good think before proceeding.

In either case, you are ahead of the game. You now know the importance of developing a clear vision, how to become a focused niche player, and what is needed to get your product on the food store shelf.

How to Know If You Are Successful

Add up your revenues, deduct your costs, and if something is left over, you might be successful.

This is the traditional means of determining success in business. A better, more long-term way, is to measure the effectiveness you and your company are having on your customers. Have you, in fact, delighted them?

There are tools you can use to measure your efforts at quality planning, and exceeding your customer's quality needs. The Malcolm Baldrige National Quality Award, administered by the U.S. Department of Commerce, incorporates criteria that you can use to evaluate your forward movement. The award was established in 1987 to promote awareness of the importance of quality improvement, to recognize organizations that made substantial improvements in competitive performance, and to foster sharing of best practice information among U.S. organizations.

The following is a brief summary of the key elements of the Malcom Baldrige National Quality Award criteria:

Leadership. This category examines how you and your key managers create and sustain clear quality values, and whether you have developed an appropriate supporting management system that promotes management excellence. An example of a quality value is your willingness to treat all customers equally. Another is to involve all members of your team in your product development and promotion planning. If you do it all alone, you suffer the chance of someone on whom you rely not having a stake in the outcome and, therefore, not giving his or her share of the effort.

Questions to ask yourself. Do you create and reinforce high expectations throughout your company? Describe your personal involvement in setting directions and in developing and maintaining a leadership system that fosters excellence. Do you set performance goals and measures through strategic planning? Do you maintain a climate conducive to continuous learning?

Information and analysis. This category examines the use of data and information to support overall performance excellence.

Questions to ask yourself. Are you in regular contact with your customers to obtain data on their needs? Do you use data as a basis for making decisions, or are you a seat-of-the-pants decision-maker? The food industry tends to be product-driven: "We grow it in Kansas, we can sell it anywhere." This is a short-sighted approach that ignores the importance of the voice of the customer. A market-driven company will succeed because it uses information gained from listening to the customer.

Strategic quality planning. This looks at how you set strategic direction, and how you determine key planning requirements.

> **CASE IN POINT**
>
> *The King's Cupboard— Company started by a husband and wife team who are molecular biologists in Red Lodge, Montana. They loved Montana and wanted to start a business so they could stay there. The company produces very high-end chocolate sauces that retail for around $8. In business for eight years, and successful at the four-year mark.*

Questions to ask yourself. Describe your strategic planning process and how this process determines and addresses key customer performance requirements. One might be rapid turn around of orders. Do you translate these requirements into critical success factors (24-hour order processing, for example)?

Human resource utilization. Examines how your sales, operations, and administrative staff are aligned with your company's overall performance objectives. Also examined are your efforts to build and maintain a climate conducive to performance excellence, full participation, and personal growth.

Questions to ask yourself. Are your resource planning and evaluation aligned with your company's overall performance improvement plan? Describe the training in quality concepts you provide for your sales, operations, and administrative staff. Do you evaluate your sales staff, for example, on how effectively it meets customer needs, as opposed to just the number of sales made? Do you reward high performing individuals or high performing teams? Do you treat your employees as costs to be reduced or assets to be developed?

> ### CASE IN POINT
>
> *Marakesh Express—The company developed a bean cuisine concept consisting of low-fat and healthy products. They had it co-packed in beautiful packages, and sold it to retailers and distributors. They hit the market at a time when Mediterranean foods were in demand. They extended the line, and hit the $2 million sales mark in about two years. Sold the company and brand to top-25 food company.*

Business process management. Key aspects of process management are examined, including design and delivery of services and business operations.

Questions to ask yourself. Describe how you develop new products, or line extensions, in response to customer needs. Is current information on customer requirements disseminated to the employees responsible for product development and improvement? Do you involve everyone in discussing possible alternatives?

Performance results. Examines your company's results (outcomes) in terms of how you met your customer needs.

Questions to ask yourself. How do you measure your success? Some ways are: return on investment, stockholder equity, gross profit margin, gross revenues, trends, number of repeat orders, new customers, complimentary letters, low employee turnover.

Customer satisfaction. Examines how you determine customer (both internal and external) satisfaction. Your primary customers (those without whom you would not exist) are the food consumers. Other customers include companies who buy your products for resale (distributors and retailers), your employees, and any other entity for whom your company provides a product or service.

Questions to ask yourself. How do you develop and maintain awareness of the needs and expectations of your current and future customers? Understanding the voice of the customer is essential to achieving customer satisfaction.

The Deming Chain Reaction

Dr. W. E. Deming—considered one of the first leaders in the global quality movement—noted that when we focus on quality, our operating costs will be reduced and our productivity will improve. The process he described is a very simple chain reaction and can be best shown in the following chart, Figure 5.1.

> **CASE IN POINT**
>
> *Selma's Cookies—1993 Outstanding Cookie: Chocolate Chip Cookie Supreme. Business started in May 1990 and is still running. Owner reports start-up costs of $10,000. Says she is successful and defines that as: "Happy customers and happy employees!" Uses Internet for sales and marketing. Offers this to newcomers: "You can do anything you want!! Just work!"*

FIGURE 5.1: **The Deming Chain Reaction**

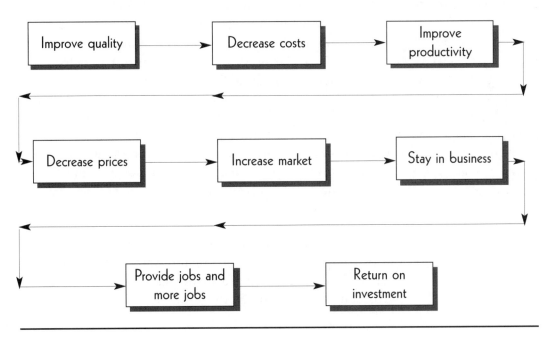

CASE IN POINT

The Initial Investment Is JUST the Beginning

The Elegant Apricot—1993 Outstanding Jam, Preserve, Spread, or Topping: Apricot Pepper Jelly. This company is part of Martin Family Farms in California. Founder Jo Martin reports that they experienced a big sales surge after winning the award, then a big fall off. They were unprepared for success. Today her focus is mostly on sun dried tomatoes, specifically, supplying other processors. She stopped exhibiting at fancy food shows and focused on marketing her farm's tomatoes. She advises that newcomers must also be prepared to take the next big step. Think about alternative ways of getting into the grocery chains. Think outside of the box; i.e., don't overdo one's own version of the elegant apricot concept.

When you focus on quality, you can improve the quality of your product, reduce its price, expand your market, and reap the profits.

Cultivating Effective Habits

If you have decided to go ahead, then take a lead from Stephen Covey's book, *The Seven Habits of Highly Effective People* (Simon and Schuster, New York, 1990), and incorporate these habits into your repertoire:

Habit 1: *Be proactive.* Proactive people develop the ability to choose their response, making them more a product of their values and decisions than their moods and conditions.

Habit 2: *Begin with the end in mind.* Effective people realize that things are created mentally before they are created physically. They write a vision or purpose statement and use it as a frame of reference for making future decisions. They clarify values and set priorities before selecting goals and going about the work.

Habit 3: *Put first things first.* To leverage our time, we should devote less attention to activities that are urgent but unimportant, more time to those things that are important but not necessarily urgent. Use your business plan to help you keep on track.

Habit 4: *Think win-win.* Effective people model the win-win principle in their relationships and agreements. The win-win performance agreement clarifies expectations by making the following five elements very explicit: desired results, guidelines, resources, accountability, and consequences.

Habit 5: *Seek first to understand, then to be understood.* We see the world as we are, not as it is. Our perceptions come out of our experiences. Most credibility problems begin with perception differences. To resolve these differences and to restore credibility, one must exercise empathy, seeking first to understand the point of view of the other person. Remember to operate for the convenience of your customer.

> Gourmet food marketing, like the frog, can be dissected, but in the process, the beast dies.

Habit 6: *Synergize.* This is the habit of creative cooperation or teamwork. For those who have a win-win abundance mentality and exercise empathy, differences in any relationship can produce synergy, where the whole is greater than the sum of its parts.

Habit 7: *Sharpen the saw.* The habit of sharpening the saw regularly means having a balanced, systematic program for self-renewal in the four areas of our lives: physical, mental, emotional-social, and spiritual.

Take these seven habits to heart. They will be useful in everything you do.

✧　✧　✧

Throughout this book, I have tried to make sense of some of the more complex issues of specialty food cost accounting, market research, pricing, and distribution. The rest of it—production, packaging, and labeling, for example—are all pretty matter of fact, save the visceral issues of what is or is not aesthetically appealing.

Ultimately, you will have to just put your foot in the water. To paraphrase a famous saying, "Gourmet food marketing, like the frog, can be dissected, but in the process, the beast dies." Death by analysis. If you have that fire in your belly, and if you have the willpower, perseverance, motivation, focus, and self-discipline . . . and if you have the money, and the health, the idea, the concept, the fever, and the VISION . . . then do it and good profits to you!

I invite you to comment on this book, and/or to make any recommendations for future editions. If you are a service provider, please submit your company name and description of your service to be considered for listing in the next edition of *From Kitchen to Market*. Send comments to:

Stephen F. Hall
c/o Dearborn Trade, A Kaplan Professional Company
155 North Wacker Drive
Chicago, IL 60606
800-621-9621

Trade Journals

The following list is neither conclusive nor is it meant to serve as an endorsement. Ask for sample copies and rate sheets.

Fancy Food & Culinary Products
20 North Wacker Drive, #1865
Chicago, IL 60606
312-849-2220; Fax: 312-849-2174
Web site: <fancyfoodmagazine.com>
e-mail: fancyfood@aol.com

Primary focus: Specialty food and gourmet food products

Food Distribution Magazine (FDM)
POB 811768
Boca Raton, FL 33481-1768
561-447-0810; Fax: 561-368-9125
e-mail: jimprevor@aol.com

Primary focus: Specialty food. Targets distributors, brokers, supermarket chain specialty food buyers, independent super-markets, and specialty and gourmet food stores.

Gift Basket Review Magazine
815 Haines Street
Jacksonville, FL 32206
904-634-1903; Fax: 904-633-8764
Web site: <www.festivities-pub.com>

Primary focus: Gift basket marketing and promotion. Design features, tips, industry news, and new products.

Gourmet Business Magazine
3300 N. Central Avenue, Suite 2500
Phoenix, AZ 85067
480-990-1101; Fax: 480-990-0819
e-mail: vpico.com

Primary focus: Retail segments of the gourmet and specialty food industry. Dedicated to bringing product trend, news, and business specific information to the gourmet retail market.

Gourmet News
POB 1056
106 Lafayette Street
Yarmouth, ME 04096
207-846-0600; Fax: 207-846-0657
Web site: <www.gourmetnews.com>
e-mail: awolfe@gourmetnews.com

Primary focus: "The business newspaper for the gourmet industry." Reports timely and newsworthy stories and events, issues, trends, and other happenings among the specialty food and natural food retailers, supermarkets, department stores, specialty distributors, and suppliers to the trade.

The Gourmet Retailer Magazine
Specialty Media, Inc.
3301 Ponce de Leon Boulevard, #300
Coral Gables, FL 33134
305-446-3388, 800-397-1137
Fax: 305-446-2868
e-mail: gourmetretailer@worldnet.att.net

Primary focus: A monthly trade publication that blends coverage of specialty food, kitchenware, coffee, and tea in a comprehensive source of news and information about the industry.

NASFT Showcase
120 Wall Street
New York, NY 10015
212-482-6440, 800-627-3869
Fax: 212-482-6459
e-mail: lstefanofs@nasft.org

Primary focus: Specialty food. Strong retailer emphasis.

Organic & Natural News
Virgo Publishing Company
POB 40079
Phoenix, AZ 86067-0079
480-990-1101; Fax: 480-990-0819
Web site: <www.organicandnaturalnews.com>
e-mail: onn@vpico.com

Primary focus: Focuses exclusively on organic and natural products. It delivers informative news and analysis about the organic and natural products market to buyers and owners of retail operations selling these products, including specialty grocers, health food stores, and mass market grocery stores.

Prepared Foods
Delta Communications, Inc.
455 N. Cityfront Plaza Drive
Chicago, IL 60611
312-222-2000

Primary focus: Grocery Trade, with a new products news section

Trade Associations

This list is neither conclusive nor is it meant to serve as an endorsement. Some references will be of minimal value to the food entrepreneur, but I have included them on the outside chance that one might be of interest.

General

**American Association of
Exporters and Importers**
11 West 42nd St., 30th Floor
New York, NY 10036-8002
212-944-2230; Fax: 212-382-2606

American Culinary Federation
POB 3466
St. Augustine, FL 32085
800-624-9458; Fax: 904-825-4758
Web site: <www.acfchefs.org>
e-mail: acp@acfchefs.net

American Frozen Food Institute
2000 Corporate Ridge, Suite 1000
McLean, VA 22102
703-821-1350; Fax: 703-821-1350

American Institute of Food Distribution Inc.
28–12 Broadway
Fair Lawn, NJ 07410-5570
201-791-5570; Fax: 201-791-5222

American Institute of Wine & Food
1550 Bryant St., #700
San Francisco, CA 94103
415-255-3000; Fax: 415-255-2874

**American Wholesale
Marketers Association**
1128 16th St. NW
Washington, DC 20036-4808
202-463-2124; Fax: 202-467-0559
Web site: <www.awmanet.org>
e-mail: info@awmanet.org

Association of Food Industries
5 Ravine Dr., #3
Matawan, NJ 07747
908-583-8188; Fax: 908-583-0798

Canned Food Information Council
500 N. Michigan Avenue
Chicago, IL 60611
312-836-7279; Fax: 312-836-6060

**Dairy & Food Industries
Supply Association (DFISA)**
1451 Dolly Madison Blvd.
McLean, VA 22101-3850
703-761-2600; Fax: 703-761-4334

**The Food Institute American
Institute of Food Distribution, Inc.**
28–12 Broadway
Fair Lawn, NJ 07410
201-791-5570; Fax: 201-791-5222
Web site: <www.foodinstitute.com>
e-mail: 70473.741@compuserve.com

Contacts: Rick Pfaff, President or Ivy
Ellenberg, Marketing Coordinator

The Food Institute is a trade association and
information reporting organization that follows trends, changing legislation, and market
statistics in the food industry. It publishes the
weekly *Food Institute Report* and numerous
food-related reports including *Food Retailing
Review, Food Mergers & Acquisitions,
Complying with the Nutritional Labeling &
Education Act, Food Markets in Review,
Supermarket Analysis Series* and much more.

Food Marketing Institute
800 Connecticut Avenue NW, #400
Washington, DC 20006
202-452-8444; Fax: 202-429-4519
Web site: <www.fmi.org>
e-mail: fmi@fmi.org

The Food Marketing Institute is a nonprofit
association conducting programs in
research, education, and public affairs on
behalf of its 1,600 members, composed
largely of multi-store chains, small regional
firms, and independent supermarkets.

**The Grocery Manufacturers of America Inc.
(GMA)**
1010 Wisconsin Avenue NW, Suite 800
Washington, DC 20007
202-337-9400; Fax: 202-337-4508
Web site: <www.gmabrands.com>
e-mail: info@gmabrands.com

GMA is a trade association of the manufacturers and processors of food and non-food
products sold primarily in retail grocery
stores in the United States. Readers may
wish to request a copy of the 1997 publication: "Efficient New Item Introduction:
Myths, Facts, and Opportunities." The goal
of this report, produced by GMA in conjunction with Ernst & Young LLP and
Progressive Grocer, is to describe techniques
for new product introduction. This study is
published with the intent of advancing the
understanding of distributors, brokers, and
manufacturers within the grocery industry in
this process. The publication is 46 pages
and available to non-members for $50,
members for $25.

Institute of Food Technologists
221 North LaSalle Street, Suite 300
Chicago, IL 60601-1401
312-782-8424; Fax: 312-782-8348
Web site: <www.ift.org>
e-mail: info@ift.org

**International Association of Culinary
Professionals**
304 West Liberty, #201
Louisville, KY 40202
502-581-9786; Fax: 502-589-3602
Web site: <www.iacp-online.org>
e-mail: iacp@hqtrs.com

International Foodservice Manufacturers Association
180 North Stetson Avenue, Suite 4400
Chicago, IL 60601-6710
312-540-4400; Fax: 312-540-4401
Web site: <www.ifmaworld.com>
e-mail: ifma@ifmaworld.com

Kosherfest
241 West 30th Street
New York, NY 10001
212-643-1623; Fax: 212-643-9164
Web site: <www.kosherfest.com>
e-mail: info@kosherchannelone.com

National-American Wholesale Grocers' Association/International Foodservice Distributors Association (NAWGA-IFDA)
201 Park Washington Court
Falls Church, VA 22046
703-532-9400; Fax: 703-538-4673

National Association for the Specialty Food Trade (NASFT)
120 Wall Street, 27th Floor
New York, NY 10005-4001
212-482-6440 or 800-627-3869 (outside NY)
Fax: 212-482-6459
Web site: <www.fancyfoodshows.com>
e-mail: custserv@fancyfoodshows.com

The NASFT is a nonprofit business trade organization that has been fostering trade, commerce, and interest in the specialty food industry since 1952. It has more than 1,800 U.S. and overseas members composed of food manufacturers, importers, distributors, and brokers involved in marketing specialty foods and beverages, fine confections, wine,

cooking accessories and publications. The association sponsors two major annual trade shows and an educational conference, and publishes *Showcase* magazine, which tracks industry trends, processor and retailer profiles, and pertinent government rules and regulations.

Specialty Food Distributors and Manufacturers Association (SFDMA)
401 North Michigan Avenue
Chicago, IL 60611
312-644-6610; Fax: 312-321-6869

National Food Processors Association
1401 New York Ave. NW
Washington, DC 20005
202-639-5900; Fax: 202-639-5932
Web site: <www.nfpa.food.org>

A primary scientific and technical association of the food industry, the National Food Processors Association (NFPA) has more than 85 years of experience and expertise in food issues. NFPA members manufacture the nation's processed-packaged fruits and vegetables, juices and drinks, meat and poultry, seafood, and specialty products.

The Food Processors Institute is the nonprofit education arm of the NFPA. Its primary educational goal is to provide a curricula of workshops, seminars, materials, texts, and leadership training in support of the food processing industry.

Member dues in NFPA start at $2,500 per year, and go up depending on member company annual revenues.

National Frozen Food Association
4755 Linglestown Road, Suite 300
Harrisburg, PA 17112-0069
717-657-8601; Fax: 717-657-9862
Web site: <www.nffa.org>
e-mail: info@nffa.org

National Grocers Association
1825 Samuel Morse Drive
Reston, VA 22090-5317
703-437-5300; Fax: 703-437-7768
Web site: <www.nationalgrocers.org>
e-mail: info@nationalgrocers.org

**National Restaurant
Association (NRA) Headquarters**
1200 17th Street NW
Washington, DC 20036-3006
202-331-5900; Fax: 202-347-2989
Web site: <www.restaurant.org>

**National Restaurant Association (NRA)
Convention Office**
150 North Michigan Avenue, Suite 2000
Chicago, IL 60601
312-853-2525; Fax: 312-853-2548

**Private Label Manufacturers
Association (PLMA)**
369 Lexington Avenue
New York, NY 10017
212-972-3131; Fax: 212-983-1382
Web site: <www.plma.com>

Baking

American Bakers Association
1350 I Street NW, #1209
Washington, DC 20005-3305
202-789-0300; Fax: 202-898-1164

Web site: <www.americanbakers.org>
e-mail: info@americanbakers.org

American Institute of Baking
1213 Baker's Way
Manhattan, KS 66502
785-537-4750; Fax: 785-537-1493
Web site: <www.aibonline.com>

Retailer's Bakery Association
14239 Park Center Drive
Laurel, MD 20707
301-725-2149; Fax: 301-725-2187

Beans/Legumes

California Dry Bean Advisory Board
531–D North Alta Avenue
Dinuba, CA 93618
209-591-4866; Fax: 209-591-5744

Idaho Bean Commission
P. O. Box 2556
Boise, ID 83701-2556
208-334-3520; Fax: 208-334-2442
Web site: <www.state.id.us/bean/>
e-mail: rtway@bean.state.id.us

USA Dry Pea & Lentil Council
2780 West Pullman Road
Moscow, ID 83843
208-882-3023; Fax: 208-882-6406
Web site: <www.pea-lentil.com>
e-mail: pulse@pea-lentil.com

Beverages

INTERBEV
1101 16th Street NW
Washington, DC 20036
202-463-6795; Fax: 202-833-2484

International Bottled Water Association
1700 Diagonal Road, Suite 650
Alexandria, VA 22314
703-683-5213; Fax: 703-683-4074

National Soft Drink Association
1101 16th Street NW
Washington, DC 20036
202-463-6732; Fax: 202-463-8277
Web site: <www.nsda.org>
e-mail: mcavanagh@nsda.com

New York Wine & Grape Foundation
350 Elm Street
Penn Yan, NY 14527
315-536-7442; Fax: 315-536-0719
Web site: <www.nywine.com>

Wine Institute
1127 Eleventh Street, Suite 900
San Francisco, CA 95814
916-441-6974; Fax: 916-441-7890
Web site: <www.wineinstitute.org>

Cheese/Dairy

American Cheese Society
1523 Judah
San Francisco, CA 94122
415-661-3844; Fax: 415-661-9708

American Dairy Association
10255 West Higgins Road, #900
Rosemont, IL 60018-5616
708-803-2000; Fax: 708-803-2077
Web site: <www.realseal.com/home.html>

American Dairy Products Institute
300 W. Washington Street, Suite 400
Chicago, IL 60606-1823
312-782-4888; Fax: 312-782-5299

Web site: <www.americandairyproducts.com>

Calcium Information Center
c/o Nutrition Information Center
515 East 71st Street, S-904
New York, NY 10021
800-321-2681; Fax: 212-746-8310

California Milk Advisory Board
400 Oyster Point Blvd., Suite 214
South San Francisco, CA 94080
650-871-6455; Fax: 650-583-7328
Web site: <www.calif-dairy.com>

Canadian Dairy Commission
1525 Carling Avenue, Suite 408
Ottawa, Canada K1A 0Z2
613-998-9490; Fax: 613-998-4492

Cheese Importers Association
460 Park Avenue, 11th Floor
New York, NY 10036
212-753-7500; Fax: 212-688-2870

Dairy Management O'Hare
International Center
10255 West Higgins Road, Suite 900
Rosemont, IL 60018-5616
708-803-2000; Fax: 708-803-2077

Eastern Dairy Deli Association
411 Route 17 S., #320
Hasbrook Heights, NJ 07604
201-288-5454; Fax: 201-288-5422

International Dairy-Deli-Bakery Association
313 Price Place, #202
P. O. Box 5528
Madison, WI 53705
608-238-7908; Fax: 608-238-6330

Web site: <www.iddanet.org>
e-mail: iddba@iddba.org

**International Dairy Foods Association,
Milk Industry Foundation, National Cheese
Institute, International Ice Cream
Association, American Butter Institute**
1250 H Street N W, Suite 900
Washington, DC 20005
202-737-4332; Fax: 202-331-7820

National Dairy Council
10255 West Higgins Road, #900
Rosemont, IL 60018-5616
708-803-2000; Fax: 708-803-2077

National Dairy Council of Canada
221 Laurier Avenue East
Ottawa, Ontario, Canada K1N 6P1
613-238-4116; Fax: 613-238-6247
Web site: <www.ndcc.ca/english/main.htm>

**New England Dairy-Deli-Bakery
Association**
400 Washington Street, #106
Braintree, MA 02184
617-849-1334; Fax: 617-849-0821

Switzerland Cheese Association
704 Executive Boulevard
Valley Cottage, NY 10989
914-268-2460; Fax: 914-268-2480

Western Dairy Council
12450 North Washington
Thornton, CO 80241
303-451-7711; Fax: 303-452-5484

Wisconsin Cheesemakers Association
3 South Pinckney, #620
Madison, WI 53703
608-255-2027; Fax: 608-255-4434
Web site: <www.wischeesemakersassn.org>
e-mail: office@wischeesemakersassn.org

Wisconsin Milk Marketing Board
8418 Excelsior Drive
Madison, WI 53717
609-836-8820; Fax: 608-836-5822

Coffee

National Coffee Association (NCA)
110 Wall Street
New York, NY 10005
212-344-5596; Fax: 212-425-7059

**National Specialty Coffee Association of
America (SCAA)**
One World Trade Center, #800
Long Beach, CA 90831
310-983-8090; Fax: 310-983-8091

Specialty Coffee Association of America
One World Trade Center, Suite 1200
Long Beach, CA 90831-1200
562-624-4100; Fax: 562-624-4101
Web site: <www.scaa.org>

Confections

Chocolate Manufacturers Association (CMA)
7900 Westpark Drive, #A–320
McLean, VA 22102
703-790-5011; Fax: 703-790-5752

Confections West, Confections
South and Confections Midwest
P. O. Box 8306
Radnor, PA 19087-8306
610-687-3426; Fax: 610-687-3426

National Confectioners Association
7900 Westpark Drive, #A-320
McLean, VA 22102
702-790-5750; Fax: 703-790-5752

Philadelphia National Candy,
Gift & Gourmet Show
651 Allendale Road
King of Prussia, PA 19406
610-265-4688; Fax: 610-265-4689

Fish/Seafood

Alaska Seafood Marketing Institute
1111 West Eighth Street, #100
Juneau, AK 99801-1895
907-465-5560; Fax: 907-465-5572

California Seafood Council
P. O. Box 91540
Santa Barbara, CA 93190-1540
805-568-3811; Fax: 805-965-5840

Catfish Farmers of America
1100 Highway 82 East, #202
Indianola, MS 38751
601-887-2699; Fax: 601-887-6857

Halibut Association of North America
P. O. Box 20717
Seattle, WA 98102
206-325-3413 or 206-324-7590

National Fisheries Institute
1525 Wilson Boulevard, #500
Arlington, VA 22209
703-524-8880; Fax: 703-524-4619

Flavors

Flavor & Extract Manufacturers Association
1620 I Street NW, #925
Washington, DC 20006
202-293-5800; Fax: 202-463-8998

National Association of Fruits,
Flavors & Syrups
5 Ravine Drive, #3
Matawan, NJ 07747
908-583-8272; Fax: 908-583-0798

Fruit

Calavo Growers of California
15661 Red Hill Avenue
Tustin, CA 92680
714-259-1166; Fax: 714-259-4810

California Apricot Advisory Board
1280 Boulevard Way, #107
Walnut Creek, CA 94595
510-937-3660; Fax: 510-937-0118

California Dried Fig Advisory Board
P. O. Box 709
Fresno, CA 93712
209-445-5626; Fax: 209-224-3449

California Kiwifruit Commission
1540 River Park Drive
Sacramento, CA 95815
916-924-0530; Fax: 916-929-3740

California Strawberry Commission
P. O. Box 269
Watsonville, CA 95077
408-724-1301; Fax: 408-724-5973
Web site: <www.calstrawberry.com>
e-mail: info@calstrawberry.com

California Table Grape Commission
392 W. Fallbrook, #101
Fresno, CA 93711
559-447-8350; Fax: 559-224-9184
Web site: <www.tablegrape.com>
e-mail: info@tablegrape.com

California Tree Fruit Agreement
975 I Street, P. O. Box 968
Reedley, CA 93654
559-638-8260; Fax: 559-638-8842
Web site: <www.caltreefruit.com>
e-mail: info@caltreefruit.com

Cherry Marketing Institute
2220 University Park Drive
Okemos, MI 48864
517-347-0010; Fax: 517-347-0605
Web site: <www.cherrymkt.org>

Cape Cod Cranberry Growers,
Cranberry Institute,
Cranberry Marketing Committee
P. O. Box 535
East Wareham, MA 02538
508-295-4132; Fax: 508-291-1511

Dried Fruit Association of California
POB 270A
Santa Clara, CA 95052
408-727-9302; Fax: 408-790-3833

New Zealand Kiwifruit
2001 W. Garfield, Pier 90
Seattle, WA 98119
604-284-1705; Fax: 604-282-0533
Web site: <www.zespri-usa.com>
e-mail: zespri@oppy.com

North American Blueberry Council
4995 Golden Foothill Parkway, Suite 2
El Dorado Hills, CA 95762
916-933-9399; Fax: 916-933-9777
Web site: <www. Bluberry.org/nabcmain-page.html>
e-mail: bberry@blueberry.org

Oregon Cherry Growers
1520 Woodrow St. NE, POB 7357
Salem, OR 97303
503-296-5487; Fax: 503-296-2509
Web site: <www.oregoncherries.com>
e-mail: mrm@orcherry.com

Oregon Blueberry Commission,
Oregon Raspberry and Blackberry
Commission, Oregon Strawberry
Commission
712 NW Fourth St.
Corvallis, OR 97330
503-758-4043; Fax: 503-758-4553

National Watermelon Promotion Board
POB 140065
Orlando, FL 32814-0065
407-895-5100; Fax: 407-895-5022

Processed Apples Institute
5775 Peachtree-Dunwoody Rd., #500-G
Atlanta, GA 30342

404-252-3663; Fax: 404-252-0774
Web site: <www.appleproducts.org>
e-mail: info@appleproducts.org

Raisin Administrative Committee
3445 N. 1st Street
Fresno, CA 93726
559-225-0520; Fax: 559-225-0652
Web site: <www.raisons.org>
e-mail: info@raisins.org

Washington Red Raspberry Commission
1626 N. Atlantic
Spokane, WA 99205
509-328-7307

Washington State Apple Commission
POB 18
Wenatchee, WA 98807
509-663-9600; Fax: 509-662-5824

**Wild Blueberry Association of
North America (WBANA)**
50 Cottage Street
Bar Harbor, ME 04609
800-233-9453; Fax: 207-288-2656
Web site: <www.wildblueberries.com>
e-mail: info@wildblueberries.com

Grain

**California Wild Rice Advisory Board
c/o The Thacker Group**
1008 Second Street, Courtyard Level
Old Sacramento, CA 95814
916-444-8363; Fax: 916-444-3536

Flax Council of Canada
465-167 Lombard Avenue

Winnipeg, Manitoba, Canada R3B 0T6
204-982-2115; Fax: 204-942-1841
Web site: <www.flaxcouncil.ca>
e-mail: flax@flaxcouncil.ca

Kansas Wheat Commission
2630 Claflin Road
Manhattan, KS 66502-2743
785-539-0255; Fax: 785-539-8946
Web site: <www.kwheat.com>
e-mail: dfrey@kswheat.com

USA Rice Federation
Houston, TX 77074
713-270-6699; Fax: 713-270-9021
Web site: <www.usarice.com>
e-mail: riceinfo@tx.usarice.com

Wheat Foods Council
10841 S. Crossroads Drive, 105
Parker, CO 80138
303-840-8737; Fax: 303-840-6877
Web site: <www.wheatfoods.olrg>
e-mail: wfc@wheatfoods.org

Hot & Spicy

Chili Institute
Box 30003, Department 3Q
Las Cruces, NM 88003
505-646-3028; Fax: 505-646-6041
Web site: <www.chilipepperinstitute.org>
e-mail: hotchile@nmsu.edu

National Hot Pepper Association
400 NW 20th Street
Fort Lauderdale, FL 33311
305-565-4972; Fax: 305-566-2208

Jams/Jellies/Preserves

International Jelly & Preserve Association
5775 Peachtree-Dunwoody Road
Atlanta, GA 30342
404-252-3663; Fax: 404-252-0774
Web site: <www.jelly.org>

Nutrition/Organic/Health

American Council on Science and Health
1995 Broadway, 2nd Floor
New York, NY 10023
212-362-7044; Fax: 212-362-4919
Web site: <www.acsh.org>
e-mail: acsh@acsh.org

American Dietetic Association
216 W. Jackson Blvd.
Chicago, IL 60606
800-366-1655 (Weekday Consumer
Nutrition Hotline)
Fax: 312-899-4899
Web site: <www.eatright.org>
e-mail: exhibit@eatright.org

Human Nutrition Program
The Rockefeller University
1230 Park Avenue, Box 246
New York, NY 10021
212-746-1617; Fax: 212-746-8310
Web site: <www.nalusda.gov/fnic/>
e-mail: miller@rockefeller.edu

Hotlines

Calcium Information Center: 800-321-2681

Garlic Information Center: 800-330-5922

Olive Oil Information Center: 800-232-6548

Organic Trade Association
POB 547
Greenfield, MA 01302
413-774-7511; Fax: 413-774-6432
Web site: <www.ota.com>
e-mail: info@ota.com

Pasta

National Pasta Association
2101 Wilson Blvd., Suite 920
Arlington, VA 22201
703-841-0818; Fax: 703-528-6507
Web site: <www.ilovepasta.org>
e-mail: info@ilovepasta.org

Produce

Produce Marketing Association
POB 6036
Newark, DE 19714-6036
302-738-7100; Fax: 302-731-2409
Web site: <www.pma.com>

Salad Dressings

Association for Dressings and Sauces
5775 Peachtree-Dunwoody Road
Atlanta, GA 30342
404-252-3663; Fax: 404-252-0774
Web site: <www.dressings-sauces.org>
e-mail: ads@assahq.com

Snacks

Snack Food Association
1711 King Street, #1
Alexandria, VA 22314
800-628-1334 or 703-836-4500;
Fax: 703-836-8262
Web site: <www.sfa.org>
e-mail: sfa@sfa.org

Tea

Tea Association of the USA, Inc.
420 Lexington Avenue, #825
New York, NY 10170
212-986-9415; Fax: 212-697-8658
Web site: <www.teausa.com>

Trade Shows and Services

The following appendices list services and sources of assistance and are meant to be neither conclusive nor to serve as an endorsement.

Boston Gift Show
March and September
Boston, Massachusetts
Bayside Exposition Center
Contact: George Little Management, Inc.
10 Bank Street
White Plains, NY 10606-1954
800-272-7469; Fax 914-948-6180
Web site: <www.glmshows.com>

Chicago Gift Show
January and July
Chicago, Illinois
McCormack Place Lakeside Center
Contact: George Little Management, Inc.
10 Bank Street
White Plains, NY 10606-1954
800-272-7469; Fax 914-948-6180
Web site: <www.glmshows.com>

Both the Boston Gift Show and the Chicago Gift Show feature specialty food products that can be successfully merchandised via the gift trade. Attendees include retailers with strong purchasing power from a variety of gift, stationery, and department stores, as well as representatives from mail-order catalogs, specialty stores, craft shops, college stores, museum shops, garden centers, and gourmet stores.

The Gourmet Products Show
Los Angeles, California
Los Angeles Convention Center, April
Contact: George Little Management, Inc.
577 Airport Blvd., Suite 440
Burlingame, CA 94010-2020
650-344-5171; Fax: 650-344-5270
Ms. Susan G. Corwin, VP
Web site: <www.glmshows.com>

Annual exhibition of high-end quality specialty food products and cookware, kitchen gadgets, cutlery, specialty appliances, etc. Estimated 950 exhibitors with 9,000 attendees in 1999.

**International Gift Basket,
Floral and Balloon Jubilee!**
Contact: Festivities Publications, Inc.
815 Haines Street
Jacksonsville, FL 32206
904-634-1903
Web site: <www. Festivities-pub.com>

**International Fancy Food
and Confection Show**
Contact: NASFT
120 Wall Street
New York, NY 10018
212-482-6440, 800-627-3869;
Fax: 212-482-6459
e-mail: lstefanofs@nasft.org

These are owned and sponsored by the
National Association for the Specialty Food
Trade (NASFT), the largest association in
the United States specializing in the representation and promotion of specialty food
and confectionery products. It sponsors
three very important annual food shows
for its members, which attract buyers and
decision-makers from all segments of the
specialty food industry. The association also
sponsors food processor seminars devoted to
food marketing and distribution issues.

NGA Annual Convention
National Grocers Association (NGA)
1825 Samuel Morse Drive
Reston, VA 22090-5317
703-437-5300; Fax: 703-437-7768
Web site: <www.nationalgrocers.org>

The NGA is the national trade association
exclusively representing the retail and
wholesale grocers who comprise the independent sector of the food distribution
industry.

Natural Products Expo
Contact: New Hope Communications
1401 Pearl Street
Boulder, CO 80302
303-939-8440; Fax: 303-939-8440
Web site: <www.naturalproductexpo.com>

The nation's largest natural products trade
show: EXPO East held in Baltimore,
Maryland in the Fall; and EXPO West held
in Anaheim, California in the Spring. Over
1,300 exhibit booths brimming with everything from grocery and personal care products to supplements and organics. Plus an
extensive seminar program featuring the
industry's top speakers.

**Philadelphia National Candy,
Gift and Gourmet Show**
651 Allendale Road
King of Prussia, PA 19406
610-265-4688 or 610-369-1044

Sponsored by the Retail Confectioners
Association of Philadelphia

Canadian Fine Food Show
Meteor Show Productions
International Centre
6900 Airport Road
Toronto, Canada
416-229-2060; Fax: 416-223-2826
e-mail: weil@meteorshows.com

Canada's national show for the specialty
food industry.

ANUGA (American Foods Pavilion)
World Food Market
Cologne, Germany
Contact: USDA, Room 4939
Washington, DC 20250-1000
202-720-7420
Web site: <www.fas.usda.gov>

Show held in October, odd-numbered years.

SIAL (American Foods Pavilion)
39, Rue de la Bienfaisance
75008, Paris, France
202-720-3425
Web site: <www.fas.usda.gov>

Show held in October, even-numbered years.
SIAL and ANUGA are biannual food shows
that are particularly beneficial to European
producers desiring to introduce products to
the United States, and for U.S. producers
wishing to export products to European
markets. Average cost for a booth in the
American Pavilion at SIAL is $11,300. Use
the Web sites, above, for initial contact.
USDA employs one of those wonderfully
convoluted telephone answering systems
that generally requires making a long-dis-
tance telephone call, listening to a listing of
options, and then getting a voice messaging
system.

In addition to SIAL and ANUGA, noted
above, their are numerous other international
trade promotion events that may be of some
value to food producers ready to explore
international markets. Contact the Foreign
Agricultural Service, USDA, Room 4647,
South Building, Washington, DC 20250-
1000, 202-690-1182; Fax: 202-690-4374.

NASDA—U.S. Food Export Showcase
National Association of
State Departments of Agriculture
1156 15th Street NW
Washington, DC 20005
202-296-9680
Contact: Convention Management Group
703-876-0900
e-mail: ammccormack@cmgexpo.com

This show is held in conjunction with the
Food Marketing Institute's Supermarket
Show.

Co-Packers

The National Association for the Specialty Food Trade (NASFT) has a listing of nearly 700 contract packaging companies (co-packers). Far too many people feel that a co-packer is a co-packer, and that any co-packer can do everything. In fact, co-packers have a variety of specific functional areas in which they excel.

Readers may wish to request that NASFT send them a co-packer listing.
Contact Ms. Heather Paul
NASFT
120 Wall Street
New York, NY 10005
800-627-3869, ext. 102 or 212-482-6440
Fax: 212-482-6459
e-mail: hpaul@nasft.org

The listing consists only of NASFT members who have indicated to the NASFT that they are co-packers. It includes the co-packer contact information, products that they co-pack, plant location, types of packaging they use, and specialized packing equipment, such as enrobers, form-fill and seal, smokers, vacuum packaging, etc.

Few co-packers can provide all of the following range of services:

♦ Liquid products

♦ Dry products

✧ Ingredient preblends

✧ Labeling

✧ Packaging service only

✧ Product development/recipe conversion

Using a qualified contract packer will enable you to devote your time to management and marketing, while eliminating the enormous expense and responsibility of operating a production facility. Some will provide only the packaging, while others will help you with the entire formulation, production, packaging, and labeling process. Most offer no-cost initial consultations. Some even have marketing capabilities. See Chapter 2 for a detailed discussion of co-packer services. Many of the companies are just food processors who have extra production capacity.

Broker Information

The following list is neither conclusive nor is it meant to serve as an endorsement.

Broker Associations

National Association of Specialty Food & Confection Brokers
175 East Delaware Place, Suite 9004
Chicago, IL 60611-7755
312-397-9494; Fax: 312-751-2497
e-mail: ExGourmet@aol.com

Request a copy of the most recent edition of their directory, which contains a specialty food broker profile. The cost is $15; make your check payable to: NASFCB.
Each broker profile includes the following information: state; company name; president; address; phone numbers; fax number; e-mail address; names of brokers in the firm; territory; customer base by type, and branch office.

National Food Brokers Association
2100 Reston Parkway, #400
Reston, VA 22091
703-758-7790; Fax: 703-758-7787

National Candy Brokers Association
710 East Ogden Avenue, Suite 113
Naperville, IL 60563
708-369-2406; Fax: 708-369-2488

Sample Broker Appointment Letter

This is a very formal version. You may use a simpler form to suit your needs.

AGREEMENT between [your company], a [corporation, proprietorship, partnership, as appropriate] ("Company"), whose principal office is located at [your address], and [broker name], a [corporation, etc., as appropriate] of [state] with principal office located at [address].

In consideration of the mutual covenants contained herein, the parties agree as follows:

Article I

APPOINTMENT
Company hereby appoints [broker name] its exclusive representative for sales of all the Company's [indicate product types, if necessary] throughout the Territory, as designated below, on the following terms and conditions.

Article II

TERRITORY
Territory means the [insert territory]. [Indicate any variations, accounts not included, etc.].

Article III

AUTHORITY
[Broker name] shall promote the sale of the Company's products according to its best judgment, including carrying out the following activities:

A. Establishing and supervising all field sales;

B. Contracting and servicing dealers, suppliers, retailers, wholesalers, and other users and purchasers for resale;

C. Assessing marketing strengths and weaknesses (prices, competition, and other contractual terms);

D. Recommending and implementing, if requested, advertising and promotional strategies and activities;

E. Receiving and transmitting orders and other requests from customers.

Article IV

RIGHT TO SOLICIT AND ACCEPT ORDERS

[Broker name]'s authority includes the exclusive right to solicit and accept orders, either directly or through its sales agents in the territory, for all products of the Company. Company agrees to transmit regularly to [broker name] all information concerning orders and sales that the Company receives or obtains directly, whether from existing customers or from third parties. [Broker name] will supply the Company its best field information on credibility for any new account and will maintain field surveillance on established accounts in terms of stability-credibility. Company has the responsibility and authority to control credit line and terms to the customer.

Article V

COMMISSION ON SALES

Unless specified otherwise:

A. [Broker name] shall be entitled on all orders shipped by the Company to a commission of 10 percent for sales to retailers, and 5 percent for sales to distributors.

B. The commission will be calculated on the total dollar amount of the order FOB [your warehouse location].

Article VI

DEVOTION OF TIME AND SKILL

A. [Broker name] agrees to use its best efforts to promote the sales and use of, and to solicit and secure orders for, the products of the Company within the Territory.

B. [Broker name] shall observe Company policies, as provided in writing by the Company, as regards the sales of Company's products and shall be furnished regularly with sales literature, technical data, and sample products by the Company, in reasonable quantities and without charge.

C. [Broker name] shall not participate in the sale of any product that would conflict with the products of the Company included in this agreement without the authorization of the Company.

Article VII

EXPENSES

Except as herein provided, [broker name] agrees to assume all expenses of its own employees, and all expenses of maintaining its organization as the sales representatives of the Company's products within the Territory and all expenses of sales agents or brokers retained by [broker name]. [Broker name] will identify and recommend advertising and promotional opportunities which, if agreed to by the Company, will be paid for by the Company.

Article VIII

COMPANIES REPRESENTED

[Broker name] will provide to the Company a list of all companies that it represents.

Article IX

DURATION OF AGREEMENT: TERMINATION

This agreement shall be effective from the execution hereof, and shall be binding on the parties hereto and their assigns, representatives, heirs, and successors. This agreement shall continue in effect for one year, and be automatically renewable annually thereafter until terminated by either party on thirty (30) days written notice to the other, provided, that in the event of insolvency or adjudication in bankruptcy or on the filing of a petition therefore by either party, this agreement may be terminated immediately at the option of either party on written notice to the other. Termination shall be without prejudice to the rights and obligations of the parties hereto that have vested prior to the effective date of termination, except that, on termination, the Company shall pay [broker name] the commissions provided only on orders received by the Company prior to the effective date of such termination and delivered to customers within ninety (90) days following the effective date of such termination. The acceptance, however, of such orders and the liability of the Company for the payment of commissions thereon are to be subject to the terms and conditions herein before provided.

Article X

CHANGES; ALTERATIONS

No change, alteration, modification or amendment to this agreement shall be effective unless in writing and properly executed by the parties hereto.

Article XI

APPLICABLE LAW

This agreement and any disputes relating thereto shall be construed under the laws of [your state], United States of America.

Article XII

CONTRACT TERMS EXCLUSIVE

This agreement constitutes the entire agreement between the parties hereto and the parties acknowledge and agree that neither of them has made any representation with respect to the subject matter of this agreement or any representations inducing the execution and delivery hereof except as specifically set forth herein and each of the parties hereto acknowledges that it has relied on its own judgment in entering into the same.

IN WITNESS WHEREOF, the parties have executed this agreement:

This _____ day of _____, 20_____

By: _____   By: _____
    (your company name)   (broker name)

_____   _____
        title   title

Catalog Sheet Preparation

These companies offer a complete package, from photography to printed sheets. You can order 2,000 to 2,500 catalog sheets with one color photograph, up to 50 words of typeset copy, color separation, and full-color printing on one side of an 80-pound coated stock for prices that range from $425 to $500, depending upon which supplier you select. Each of the following companies was invited to provide particulars as to its services. Only those that responded have descriptions beyond the name, address, and telephone number. This list is neither conclusive nor is it meant to serve as an endorsement.

Colorlith Corporation
777 Hartford Avenue
Johnston, RI 02919
800-556-7171 or 401-751-9436

Create-A-Card, Inc.
16 Brasswood Road
St. James, NY 11780
800-753-6867 (outside New York) or
631-584-2273; Fax: 631-584-3214
Web site: <www.createacardinc.com>

Primary focus: Promotion card and catalog sheet printers. Sample offering: 2,500 80-pound coated paper, 8½" by 11", full-color catalog sheets for $495 (from your disk-ready art).

Direct Press Modern Litho—Company headquarters are in Virginia. See listing below.

California
6817 E. Gage Avenue
City of Commerce, CA 90040
800-720-4098 or 562-927-7735
Fax: 562-928-3807

Connecticut
304 Main Avenue, Suite 385
Norwalk, CT 06851
888-857-9600 or 203-563-6192
Fax: 203-563-6194

Florida
4806 NE 12th Avenue
Oakland Park, FL 3334

800-415-9706 or 954-938-8070
Fax: 953-938-1118

Georgia
1670 Oakbrook Drive, Suite 385
Norcross, GA 30093
800-827-2293 or 770-840-7255
Fax: 770-840-7753

Illinois
6211 W. Howard Street
Niles, IL 60714
800-735-6622 or 847-647-6622
Fax: 847-647-0039

Maryland
7397 Washington Blvd., Unit 103
Elkridge, MD 21075
800-410-4187 or 410-796-2424
Fax: 410-796-7603

New York
155 West 23rd Street, 2nd Floor
New York, NY 10011
800-560-9491 or 212-741-8300
Fax: 212-741-8326

89 Cabot Court, Unit L
Hauppauge, NY 117788
888-563-4732 or 516-952-0300
Fax: 516-952-2159

New Jersey
34 Ludwig Street
Little Ferry, NJ 07643
800-560-8977 or 201-807-0080
Fax: 201-807-1320

Pennsylvania
4110 Butler Pike, Suite A106

Plymouth Meeting, PA 19462
800-264-8214 or 610-828-1556
Fax: 610-828-1823

Rhode Island
31 Graystone Street
Warwick, RI 02886
800-560-9495 or 401-737-2100
Fax: 401-737-2213

Texas
Century Business Park
2030 Century Center Blvd., Suite A
Irving, TX 75062
800-729-1110 or 972-721-1110
Fax: 972-438-5065

Virginia
7644 Dynatech Court
Springfield, VA 22153
800-347-3285 or 703-923-1200
Fax: 703-455-4558
Web site: <www.directpress.com>

Kenner Printing Company
418 West 25th Street
New York, NY 10001
212-463-9436

Megacolor Corporation
1380 SW 8th Street
Pompano Beach, FL 33069
888-333-8507 or 954-782-3600
Fax: 954-247-0083
Web site: <www.mcolor.com/home.htm>
e-mail: info@mcolor.com

Contact: Kory Hershkowitz
Primary focus: MegaColor specializes in
photography and full-color printing of

brochures, catalog sheets, posters, and post-cards. They guarantee the best prices and quality in the country.

Photowork
104 Brandon Road
Pleasant Hill, CA 94523
925-279-1120 or 800-937-4110
e-mail: PHOTO@DNAI.COM

Primary focus: Photowork produces afford-able advertising tools for food manufactur-ers, wholesalers, distributors, and importers. They can prepare short-run printings of postcards, trade show handout sheets, small catalogs, magazine ads, and trade show background posters. They understand the needs and budgets of small vendors. Samples and prices will be sent on request.

Packaging Design

These companies supply and design packages. This list is neither conclusive nor is it meant to serve as an endorsement.

Krepe-Kraft, Inc.
4199 Bay View Road
Blasdell, NY 14219
716-826-7086; Fax: 800-826-7239
e-mail: sales@krepekraft.com

Presentation Packaging
870 Louisiana Avenue South
Minneapolis, MN 55426-1614
800-326-2698 or 612-540-9544
Fax: 612-540-9522
Web site: <www.presentationpackaging.com>
e-mail: customerservice@presentationpack-aging.com

Contact: Carol Sylvester, Connie Maloney, and/or Lori Pearson

Primary focus: Presentation Packaging designs and manufactures imaginative corrugated packaging for the food, mail order, retail, giftware, and direct mail industries.

Company reports that its stock collection is the largest available in the industry, combining colorful pre-prints, litho-label, and direct print patterns, with a huge selection of shapes and sizes. All boxes ship and store flat.

Specialty Food Packaging Design
PBC International
One School Street, #302
Glen Cove, NY 11542
516-676-2727; Fax: 516-676-2738
e-mail: pbcintl@aol.com

This book, written by New York Public Library Culinary Collection head, Reynaldo Alejandro, in association with the NASFT, contains more than 200 examples of specialty food package design. The book may be purchased from PBC for $60 per copy. NASFT member discount is 30 percent.

Packaging and Labeling Materials

These companies are known to provide specialty food containers, labeling services, and materials. There are hundreds of others (more than five dozen exhibited at the 1999 NASFT Summer Fancy Food Show), and you should check available listings for some near you. This list is not meant to serve as an endorsement.

AKM Packaging, Inc. (No glass jars)
223 Clover Hill Drive
Feeding Hills, MA 01030
800-836-6256; Fax: 413-786-8097
Web site: <www.akmpackaging.com>
e-mail: akm5253@aol.com

Berlin Packaging
435 E. Algonquin Road
Arlington Heights, IL 60005
800-4-BERLIN (800-423-7546)
Fax: 800-423-7545
Web site: <www.berlinpackaging.com>

Specific focus: Berlin Packaging is the largest U.S. distributor of glass, plastic, and metal containers plus accompanying closure systems. Call 800-4-BERLIN for a free catalog with more than 3,100 bottles, jars, tubs, etc. All orders placed before 3:00 PM ship the same day. There are no minimum quantity requirements. Professional customer service representatives are available to answer packaging questions and help you locate the ideal container for your product.

Driscoll Label Co., Inc.
1275 Bloomfield Avenue
Fairfield, NJ 07004
973-575-8492; Fax: 800-342-1195

Label Graphics Manufacturing
175 Patterson Avenue
Little Falls, NJ 07424
201-890-5665; Fax: 201-890-1164

Labels Plus
2407 106th Street
Everett, WA 98204
206-745-4592 or 800-275-7587
Fax: 206-523-1973
Web site: <www.labelsplus.com>
e-mail: trace@labelsplus.com

Labels Unlimited
493 London Bridge Road, #103
Virginia Beach, VA 23454
757-340-8893; Fax: 757-486-8854

Specific focus: Label printing, thermal transfer.

MOD-PAC Corp.
1801 Elmwood Avenue
Buffalo, NY 14207-2496
716-873-0640, 800-666-3722
Fax: 800-873-1269

Primary focus: Quality paperboard folding cartons for every day and every season. Special stock run and custom run programs.

Olshen's Bottle Supply Co.
2331 NE Argyle Street
Portland, OR 07211
800-258-4292; Fax: 503-290-4260
Web site: <www.richardspackaginginc.com>
e-mail: trooper731@aol.com

Primary focus: A family-owned business since 1925, Olshen's distributes stock glass and plastic containers and closures. Also offers special order and design custom items.

Pohlig Brothers, Inc.
POB 2470
Chesterville, VA 23832
804-275-9000; Fax: 804-275-9900

Specific focus: Manufacture of custom designed paperboard boxes.

Polyfoam Packers
2320 South Foster Avenue
Wheeling, IL 60090
847-398-0110; Fax: 847-398-0653
Web site: <www.polyfoam.com>

Specific focus: Products for the shipment, storage, and distribution of perishables.

Presentation Packaging
870 Louisiana Avenue South
Minneapolis, MN 55426
800-328-1784 or 612-540-9544;
Fax: 612-540-9522
Web site: <www.presentationpackaging.com>

Western Specialty Container
2040 S. Lynx Place
Ontario, CA 91761
909-923-6150; Fax: 909-923-6052
Web site: <www.westernspecialty.com>
e-mail: donnak@westspec.com

Specific focus: Decorative tins, glass, and plastic containers, including PET wide-mouth jars and bottles, tamper evident bands, and a wide assortment of packaging concepts.

Internet Resources

The following list is neither conclusive nor is it meant to serve as an endorsement.

References

Easy World Wide Web with Netscape
by Jim Minatel, 1995
Que Corp., Indianapolis, IN
800-428-5331

An easy to follow, step-by-step guide with full-color illustrations and screen shots on every page. Very useful if you are browsing the World Wide Web.

The Food Channel
Web site: <www.foodchannel.com>

This World Wide Web forum provides trend information, reports, and other food-industry facts plus online forums, links to other food sites, and a direct link to Food Channel staff.

Food Net
Web site: <foodnet.fic.cal>

Useful information on North American and international food trends.

American Demographics
Web site: <www.demographics.com>

A good source of consumer trend information for business leaders.

NASFT
Web site: <www.specialty-foods.com>

The NASFT produces an online specialty food catalog that brings specialty food products directly to consumers. It does not offer the products directly, but rather connects the consumer with a search capability to more than 200 listings of specialty food companies' Web sites.

Poor Richard's E-Mail Publishing
Chris Pirillo and Peter Kent

Covers everything about e-mail publishing including the mechanics of publishing and an extensive resource directory. Top Floor Publishing. Available from Amazon.com

Web Site Development

Deep River Interactive
Web site: <www.deepriver.com>

E-Zine University: Learn to Make and Promote E-Mail Publications
Web site: <www.ezineuniversity.com>

An electronic magazine that provides information on creating and maintaining an online comprehensive newsletter.

Elfin Creative
Web site: <www.elfincreative.com>

HQ Cyberservices
Web site: <www.hqcyberservices.com>

Modern Advantage
7644 Dynatech Court
Springfield, VA 22153
800-347-1200

Modern advantage develops Web sites at Custom WebsiteDesign or Redesign. Modern Advantage handles all your company's advertising needs, from creating and placing an ad, to designing a dynamic Internet Web site. They also offer data transfer, high res scanning, CD-ROM development, poster creation, and many other features. They have a team of top designers and computer technicians to assure the very finest attention to detail. The parent company, Direct Press Modern Litho, offers a turnkey approach to four-color printing. They offer fine printing, typesetting, and photography all at a great price.

Sample Services and Pricing for Modern Advantage

Server setup fee (one time only)	$50
One year service. Includes 13 months, comes with two hours of free updates and registration with over 150 search engines.*	$360
Basic design, type, and code for each Web page	$135/page
Scans of artwork or photos not previously printed by Direct Press	$30 each
Custom animations	$100/hr.
Silhouetting of image	$15–$30
Order form	$125 +
Secure order form (for sites without shopping cart)	$175 +
Internet domain name subscription for a two-year period billed directly to you by Network Solutions.	$70
Shopping cart service via Internet partner. $10 for 0–200 transactions per month paid one year in advance. Months over 200 but less than 500 transactions is $15 additional for every month over the base of 200.	$120/yr. billed directly by our Internet partner

Page updates	$25 per 15 min.
Coding shopping cart items. Each item needs to be coded with id, price, and shipping. Options such as color, and size are $5 per option per item	$10.00 each
Pagelettes (mini pages showing an enlarged view of one item)	$30 each
Cut charge (cutting a large group photo into small ones)	$2 each

PPI
Web site: <www.paperpen.com>

Paraglyph
Web site: <www.paraglyph.com>

The Web Marketing Resource Center
Web site: <www.promotion-tips.com>

This is a free resource developed to help Web site owners, advertisers, and marketing professionals get the most from their marketing activities. The site includes details of the latest Web marketing techniques being used by many of the most successful sites on the Internet, and features articles, reviews, and links to hundreds of the best Web site promotion resources available.

Miscellaneous

Outback Plus
Web site: <www.silverlaketech.com>

This is a computer program that backs up in-boxes, out-boxes, and folders associated with Microsoft's Outlook e-mail software in a compressed archive. Available from SilverLake Tech at 973-259-9300.

Federal Government Sources

Code of Federal Regulations

The Code of Federal Regulations (CFR) contains the specific laws governing labels and ingredient statements for food products. Copies of the appropriate chapters may be purchased from your local government printing office.

Small Business Administration (SBA)
1441 L Street NW
Washington, DC 20416
800-368-5855 or 202-653-7561

The SBA provides business counseling and has a government-guaranteed loan program for small businesses. You can only qualify for such loans if you have been refused by your local bank. Don't hold your breath. Very few food entrepreneurs are able to access these funds. Ask for the address of the regional office nearest you.

Small Business Development Centers (SBDC)

Web site: <www.sbaonline.sba.gov/sbdc/>

The U.S. Small Business Administration (SBA) administers the Small Business Development Center Program to provide management assistance to current and prospective small business owners. SBDCs offer one-stop assistance to small businesses by providing a wide variety of information and guidance in central and easily accessible branch locations.

University of Alabama, Birmingham, AL 205-934-7260

University of Alaska/Anchorage, Anchorage, AK 907-274-7232

Maricopa County Community College, Tempe, AZ 602-731-8202

University of Arkansas, Little Rock, AR 501-324-9043

California Trade and Commerce Agency, Sacramento, CA 916-324-5068

Office of Business Development, Denver, CO 303-892-3809

University of Connecticut, Storrs, CT
203-486-4135

University of Delaware, Newark, DE
302-831-2747

Howard University, Washington, DC
202-806-1550

University of West Florida, Pensacola, FL
904-444-2060

University of Georgia, Athens, GA
706-542-6762

University of Hawaii at Hilo, Hilo, HI
808-933-3515

Boise State University, Boise, ID
208-385-1640

Dept. of Commerce & Community Affairs,
Springfield, IL 207-524-5856

Economic Dev. Council, Indianapolis, IN
317-264-6871

Iowa State University, Ames, IA
515-292-6351

Fort Hays State University, Hays, KS
785-296-6514

University of Kentucky, Lexington, KY
606-257-7668

Northeast Louisiana University, Monroe, LA
318-342-5506

University of Southern Maine, Portland, ME
207-780-4420

University of Maryland, College Park, MD
301-405-2147

University of Massachusetts, Amherst, MA
413-545-6301

Wayne State University, Detroit, MI
313-577-4848

Dept. of Trade and Economic Development
St. Paul, MN 612-297-5770

University of Mississippi, University, MS
601-232-5001

University of Missouri, Columbia, MO
314-882-0344

Department of Commerce, Helena, MT
406-444-4780

University of Nebraska at Omaha, Omaha,
NE 402-554-2521

University of Nevada in Reno, Reno, NV
702- 784-1717

University of New Hampshire, Durham, NH
603-862-2200

Rutgers University, Newark, NJ
201-648-5950

Santa Fe Community College, Santa Fe, NM
505-438-1362

State University of New York, Albany, NY
518-443-5398

University of North Carolina, Raleigh, NC
919-571-4154

University of North Dakota, Grand Forks, ND
701-771-3700

Dept. of Development, Columbus, OH
614-466-2711

S.E. Oklahoma State University, Durant, OK
405-924-0277

Lane Community College, Eugene, OR
503-726-2250

University of Pennsylvania, Philadelphia, PA
215-898-1219

Inter American University, Hato Rey, PR
787-763-5108

Bryant College, Smithfield, RI
401-232-6111

University of South Carolina, Columbia, SC
803-777-4907

University of South Dakota, Vermillion, SD
605-677-5498

University of Memphis, Memphis, TN
901-678-2500

Dallas Community College, Dallas, TX
214-565-5833

University of Houston, Houston, TX
713-752-8444

Texas Tech University, Lubbock, TX
806-745-3973

University of Texas at San Antonio, San
Antonio, TX 210-558-2450

Salt Lake City Community College, Salt
Lake City, UT 801-957-3481

Vermont Technical College, Randolph
Center, VT 802-728-9101

University of the Virgin Islands, St. Thomas,
US VI 809-776-3206

Dept. of Economic Development,
Richmond, VA 804-371-8258

Washington State University, Pullman, WA
509-335-1576

Governor's Office of Community and
Industrial Development, Charleston, WV
304-558-2960

University of Wisconsin, Madison, WI
608-263-7794

University of Wyoming, Laramie, WY
307-766-3505

U.S. Department of Commerce
14th and Constitution Ave.
Washington, DC 20230
202-377-2000
Web site:

You can forget about any substantive marketing assistance from this department.

Food marketing (domestic and international) is not conducted by the DOC. Check, instead, with the Department of Agriculture and its Foreign Agricultural Service.

Food and Drug Administration
International Activities Branch Center for
Food Safety and Applied Nutrition FDA
(HFS–585)
200 C Street SW
Washington, DC 20204
Web site:
<http://vm.csfan.fda.gov/label.html>

Request free copy of information on how to start a food business. Their Web page includes a lot of information, including a Food Labeling Guide.

FDA State Offices
Web site: <www.fda.gov/oca/sthealth.htm>

Their Web site will get to a complete listing of all state departments of health. These include food safety sections.

Business Services

The following listing is neither conclusive nor is it meant to serve as an endorsement.

Green Harbor Associates
4 Calypso Lane
Marshfield, MA 02050
781-837-1664; Fax: 781-837-8404
e-mail: gr.harbor@att.net

Primary focus: The firm offers a marketing-consulting service to manufacturers of specialty foods, from assisting on label design to picking a distribution channel, to an extensive marketing strategy. In addition, the firm handles all aspects of trade advertising and public relations. Interested parties are invited to contact the firm's principal, Mr. Ronald M. Cardoos.

Food Marketing & Economics Group
129 C Street
Davis, CA 95616
530-753-1632; Fax: 530-753-6113
e-mail: foodmarketing@mindspring.com

Primary focus: Market research and marketing program development for small food companies. Product experience includes energy drinks, energy bars, specialty sugar, seafood, wild rice, chili peppers, rice mixes, olives, beans, and fruit juices. Contact: Shermain Hardesty.

Lawrence-Allen Group NutriLABEL
2031 Fairmont Drive
San Mateo, CA 94402-3925
650-345-2909 or 800-609-2909
Fax: 650-345-9723
Web site: <www.nutrilabel.com>
e-mail: info@nutrilabel.com

Primary focus: Provide fast, low-cost services including food product nutritional analysis, camera-ready nutrition facts panel art, FDA labeling compliance assistance, ingredient statement preparation, trademark research, and new specialty food product development and consulting services. Confidential service with more than 50 years experience. Contact Mr. Larry Imes.

State Resources, Associations, and Agencies

This list is neither conclusive nor is it meant to serve as an endorsement. Where only state departments of agriculture are listed, be prepared to receive limited assistance. Most such departments are devoted to commodity marketing, not retail-packaged, high value, food products. In those instances where no state association is listed, you may wish to consult Appendix M: Sources of Export Assistance for a listing of State Departments of Agriculture.

State Departments of Commerce

Every state has a department of commerce and business development, usually located at the state capital. Its sole purpose is to promote and develop business within the state and offer new businesses information on state regulations and any legal requirements that apply.

States with Specialty Food Marketing Associations

CALIFORNIA
The California Specialty Food Association
c/o Mill Valley Organic and Natural Foods
905 Sir Francis Drake Blvd.
Kentfield, CA 94904
800-774-2732

Web site: <www.w2.com/docs2/act/resources/csfa/info.html>

Contact: Kiki Goshay

CONNECTICUT
Connecticut Specialty Food and Beverage Association
262 Cedar Ridge Drive
Glastonbury, CT 06033
203-633-3826

This association has published a directory of resources essential to food producers. The book includes listings of glass manufacturers, box manufacturers, basket companies, packaging and bag businesses, printers, label designers, co-packers, truckers, food technologists, public relations agencies, etc.

LOUISIANA
Louisiana Department of
Agriculture and Forestry
POB 3334
Baton Rouge, LA 70821-3334
225-922-1280; Fax: 225-922-1289
e-mail: lisa_m@ldaf.state.us

MASSACHUSETTS
Massachusetts Department of
Food and Agriculture
Division of Agricultural Development
100 Cambridge Street, 21st Floor
Boston, MA 02202
617-727-3018, ext. 172

The department provides an array of marketing support services to both value-added specialty food and agricultural producers. Options for participation in Massachusetts pavilions at trade shows, special events, seminars, and referrals are provided.

Massachusetts Specialty Food Association
POB 985
Mashpee, MA 02659
800-813-5862
Web site: <www.massgrown.org>

The association supports and strengthens specialty producers to enhance the Massachusetts economy and promotes the interest of food producers and processors in the state. It serves as an umbrella organization to assist its members in obtaining financial, scientific, management, marketing, and technical assistance. The association has access to consultation in many

fields, including research and development, business and financial management, marketing, and technical and scientific areas.

MINNESOTA
Minnesota Department of Agriculture
90 West Plato Blvd.
Saint Paul, MN 55107
651-296-7945
Web site: <www.mda.state.mn.us>

NEW MEXICO
New Mexico Food Producers and Processors
Association
POB 7310
Albuquerque, NM 87194
505-869-5605
Contact: Debbie Wilmot

NORTH CAROLINA
North Carolina Specialty Foods Association
c/o 1109 Agricultural Street
Raleigh, NC 27603
919-833-7647; Fax 919-878-0041

OHIO
Ohio Department of Agriculture
Ohio Proud
8995 East Main Street
Reynoldsburg, OH 43068
800-467-7683; Fax: 614-644-5017

SOUTH CAROLINA
South Carolina Specialty Food Products
Association
POB 21748
Charleston, SC 29413-1748
803-559-0383; Fax 803-559-3049

TEXAS
Texas Department of Agriculture
Taste of Texas Program
POB 112847
Austin, TX 78711
512-475-1663; Fax 512-463-9968
e-mail: SDUNN@AGR.STATE.TX.US

This agency has access to large database called Texas Agriculture Marketing Exchange (TAME).

VERMONT
Vermont Department of
Agriculture, Food and Markets
116 State Street
Drawer 20
Montpelier, VT 05620-2901
802-828-2416; Fax: 802-828-2361

VIRGINIA
Virginia Department of
Agriculture and Consumer Services
Division of Marketing
POB 1163
Richmond, VA 23209
804-786-4278; Fax: 804-371-6097

The Food and Libations Association of
Virginia (FLAVA)
POB 859
Williamsburg, VA 23187
804-565-4144; Fax: 804-565-4144

Sponsored by the Virginia Department of Agriculture, FLAVA offers networking opportunities, cooperative promotions, newsletter, and professional development to Virginia specialty food processors, service and product providers, and retailers.

WISCONSIN
Wisconsin Cheese and Specialty Food
Merchants Association
111 South Hamilton
Madison, WI 53703
608-255-0373; Fax: 608-255-6600

Wisconsin Specialty Cheese Institute
POB 1264
Madison, WI 53701
800-697-8861; Fax: 608-255-4434
Web site: <www.wisspecialcheese.org>

Something Special From Wisconsin Program
Wisconsin Department of Trade and
Consumer Protection
Division of Marketing
POB 8911
Madison, WI 53708-8911
608-224-5128; Fax: 608-224-5111

Export Assistance

The following organizations work with the U.S. Department of Agriculture's Foreign Agriculture Service, and are involved actively in the overseas promotion of value-added food products:

U.S. Department of Agriculture (USDA)
Foreign Agricultural Service (FAS)
AG Export Services
Washington, DC 20250-1000
202-690-3576; Fax: 202-690-0193
Web site: <www.fas.usda.gov/
startagexporting.html>
e-mail: startagexporting@fas.usda.gov

The FAS maintains a global network of agricultural counselors, attachés and officers covering more than 100 countries, to help build markets overseas, and gather and assess information on world agricultural production and trade. Its traditional focus has been on agricultural commodities, but it has recently developed a sensitivity to the market potential and longer profits associated with high value retail-packaged food products.

U.S. Department of Commerce (USDOC)
Industry and Trade Administration (ITA)
14th and Constitution Avenue NW
Washington, DC 20230
202-377-2000
Web site: <www.ita.gov>

Useful for economic and general marketing data. No food-related assistance.

Small Business Administration (SBA)
1441 L Street NW
Washington, DC 20416
800-368-5855 or 202-653-7561

Same as USDOC; generic small business export assistance. Not food-specific.

Eastern United States Agriculture Food and Export Council (EUSAFEC)
150 S. Independence Mall West, Suite 1036
Philadelphia, PA 19106
215-829-9111; Fax: 215-829-9777

EUSAFEC Members Internet Links
Web site: <www.fas.usda.gov/tapo>

Connecticut Department of Agriculture
State Office Building
Hartford, CT 06106
203-566-4845; Fax: 203-566-6094

Delaware Development Office
820 French Street
Wilmington, DE 19801
302-577-6262; Fax: 302-577-3302

Delaware Economic Development Office
99 Kings Highway
Dover, DE 19901
302-739-4271; Fax: 302-739-5749

Massachusetts Department of Food & Agriculture
100 Cambridge Street, Rm. 2103
Boston, MA 02202
617-727-3002; Fax: 617-727-7235

Maine Department of Agriculture
28 State House Station
Augusta, ME 04333
207-287-3491; Fax: 207-287-7548

New Hampshire Department of Agriculture
Caller Box 2042
Concord, NH 03302-2042
603-271-2505; Fax: 603-271-1109

New Jersey Department of Agriculture
CN 330
Trenton, NJ 08625
609-984-2279; Fax: 609-984-5367

New York Department of Agriculture
1 Winners Circle/Capital Plaza
Albany, NY 12234
518-457-7076; Fax: 518-457-2716

Pennsylvania Department of Agriculture
2301 N. Cameron Street
Harrisburg, PA 17110
717-783-3181; Fax: 717-787-1858

Rhode Island Division of Agriculture
22 Hayes Street
Providence, RI 02908
401-277-2781; Fax: 401-277-6047

Vermont Department of Agriculture
120 State Street
Montpelier, VT 05602
802-828-3827; Fax: 802-828-2361

Western U.S.A. Trade Association (WUSATA)
2500 Main Street, Suite 110
Vancouver, WA 98660
360-693-3373

WUSATA Members Internet Links
Web site: <www.wusata.org/body.html>

Alaska Department of Natural Resources
POB 949
Palmer, AK 99645-0949
907-745-7200; Fax: 907-745-7112

Arizona Department of Agriculture
1688 West Adams Street

Phoenix, AZ 85007
602-542-0982; Fax: 602-542-0969

**California Department of Food &
Agriculture**
1220 N Street, Room A280
Sacramento, CA 95814
916-654-0389; Fax: 916-653-2604
e-mail: 74404.273@compuserve.com

Colorado Department of Agriculture
700 Kipling Street, #4000
Lakewood, CO 80215-5894
303-239-4114; Fax: 303-239-4125
e-mail: CdaJimR@aol.com

Hawaii Department of Agriculture
POB 22159
1428 S. King Street
Honolulu, HI 96823-2159
808-973-9564; Fax: 808-973-9590
e-mail: CAOLIVE@PIXI-COM

Idaho Department of Agriculture
POB 790
Boise, ID 83701
208-332-8530; Fax: 208-334-2879
e-mail: lhobbs@agri.state.id.us

Montana Department of Agriculture
Capitol Station
Helena, MT 59620
406-444-2402; Fax: 406-444-5409
e-mail: ck0331%zip004@mt.gov

New Mexico Department of Agriculture
Box 5600
Las Cruces, NM 88003
505-646-4929; Fax: 505-646-3303

Oregon Department of Agriculture
121 SW Salmon Street, #240
Portland, OR 97204-2987
503-229-6734; Fax: 503-229-6113
e-mail: kvainess@oda.state.or.us

Utah Department of Agriculture
POB 146500
Salt Lake City, UT 84114-6500
801-538-7108; Fax: 801-538-7126

Washington Department of Agriculture
POB 42560
Olympia, WA 98504-2560
360-902-1933; Fax: 360-902-2089
e-mail: 74323.2112@Compuserve.com

Wyoming Department of Agriculture
2219 Carey Avenue
Cheyenne, WY 82002-0100
307-777-7321; Fax: 307-777-6593

**Middle America International Agri-Trade
Council (MIATCO)**
400 W. Erie Street, Suite 100
Chicago, IL 60201
312-944-3030

MIATCO Members Internet Links
Web site: <www.miatco.org/trade.html>

Illinois Department of Agriculture
POB 19281
Springfield, IL 62794-9281
217-782-6675; Fax: 217-524-5960

**Indiana Office of the Commissioner of
Agriculture**
One North Capitol, Suite 700

Indianapolis, IN 46204
317-233-4459; Fax: 317-232-4146

Iowa Department of Agriculture & Land Stewardship
Henry A. Wallace Building
Des Moines, IA 50319
515-242-6238; Fax: 515-242-5015

Kansas State Board of Agriculture
901 S. Kansas Avenue, Room 103
Topeka, KS 66612-1282
913-296-3736; Fax: 913-296-2247

Michigan Department of Agriculture
POB 30017
Lansing, MI 48909
517-373-1058; Fax: 517-335-7071

Minnesota Trade Office
1000 World Trade Center
30 East 7th Street
St. Paul, MN 55101
612-297-4222; Fax: 612-296-3555

Missouri Department of Agriculture
POB 630
Jefferson City, MO 65102
314-751-4338; Fax: 314-751-2868

Nebraska Department of Agriculture
POB 94947
Lincoln, NE 68509
402-471-4876; Fax: 402-471-2759

North Dakota
Department of Agriculture
600 East Blvd.
Bismark, ND 58505
701-328-2231; Fax: 701-328-4567

Ohio Department of Agriculture
International Trade Program
65 South Front Street, Room 608
Columbus, OH 43215-4193
614-752-9815; Fax: 614-644-5017

South Dakota
Department of Agriculture
445 East Capitol
Pierre, SD 57501-5436
Fax: 605-773-5926

Wisconsin Department of Agriculture
POB 8911
Madison, WI 53708
608-224-5112; Fax: 608-224-5111

Southern United States Trade Association (SUSTA)
World Trade Center, Suite 1540
2 Canal Street
New Orleans, LA 70130-1408
504-568-5986

SUSTA Members
Arkansas—Reference SUSTA listing, above

Florida Department of Agriculture & Consumer Services
Box A, Room 411, Mayo Building
Tallahassee, FL 32339-0800
904-488-4366; Fax: 904-922-0374

Georgia Department of Agriculture
Capitol Square
Atlanta, GA 30334-4201
404-656-3740; Fax: 404-656-9390

Kentucky Department of Agriculture
500 Mero Street, 7th Floor

Frankfort, KY 40601
502-564-4696; Fax: 502-564-6527

Louisiana Department of Agriculture and Forestry
POB 3334
Baton Rouge, LA 70821-3334
504-922-1280; Fax: 504-922-1289

Maryland Department of Agriculture
50 Harry S. Truman Parkway
Annapolis, MD 21401
410-841-5880

Mississippi Department of Agriculture and Commerce
POB 1609
Jackson, MS 39215
601-354-7097; Fax: 601-354-6001

North Carolina Department of Agriculture
POB 27647
Raleigh, NC 27611
919-733-7912; Fax: 919-733-0999

Oklahoma Department of Agriculture
2800 N. Lincoln Blvd.
Oklahoma City, OK 73105
800-580-6543 or 405-521-3864
Fax: 405-521-4912

South Carolina Department of Agriculture
Wade Hampton State Office Building
Box 11280
Columbia, SC 29211
803-734-2210; Fax: 803-734-2192

Tennessee Department of Agriculture
POB 40627
Nashville, TN 37204
615-360-0160; Fax: 615-360-0194

Virginia Department of Agriculture
POB 1163
Richmond, VA 23209
804-786-5867

Useful Publication

Exporter's Guide to Federal Resources for Small Business Exporters
Superintendent of Documents
U.S. Government Printing Office
World Savings Building
720 North Main Street
Pueblo, CO 81003
719-544-3142

APPENDIX N

Sample Forms

Forms Listing

Sample Application for Credit

Sample Price List/Order Form

Sample Invoice

Sample Broker Statement

Sample Statement of Account

Sample Dunning Letter 1

Sample Dunning Letter 2

Sample Dunning Letter 3

Sample Application for Credit

Application For Credit

Date: _____

Company Name: _____

Business Address: _____

_____

Mailing Address: _____

City, State, Zip: _____

Phones: _____

Type of business: _____

| Year business started: _____ | Years at present location: _____ |

Type ☐ Private Corporation   ☐ Partnership

☐ Public Corporation   ☐ Individual

Officers — Name	Position	Home Address	Phone

Banking References

1st Bank: _____

2nd Bank: _____

Trade References

1st Firm: _____

2nd Firm: _____

3rd Firm: _____

Credit Limit Requested: $ _____

In making this application for credit, the customer agrees to pay all invoices within 30 days from date of invoice and to pay a service charge of 1-1/2% per month, which is an annual percentage rate of 18% on all overdue balances. In the event a suit is necessary to collect any amount, the customer agrees to pay the seller's reasonable attorney fees and costs including attorneys fees for appeal.

Signature: _____   Title: _____   Date: _____

Sample Price List

Product or Company Name

Sales Message/Testimonial

Retailer Price List and Order Form   Date:

Cases Ordered	Description	Case Pack	Case Lbs. Shipping Wt.	Unit Price	Case Price
_____	New Gourmet Condiment	12/8 Oz. Jar	9	$ 3.75	$ 45.00
_____	New Gourmet Condiment	12/12 Oz. Jar	14	7.00	84.00

Bill To: _____   Ship To: _____

Address: _____   Address: _____

City: _____ State: ____ Zip: _____   City: _____ State: ____ Zip: _____

Special Handling Instructions: _____

Customer Order Number: _____   Your Company Number: _____

Terms: C.O.D. Until Credit Approved, then Net 30 days, F.O.B. my warehouse
       Prices subject to change without notice.

Thank You For Your Order

If available, this space should be used for more product and promotional data

My Company Name, Address, Telephone, Fax, Etc.

Sample Invoice

Your Company Name
Address
City, State, Zip
Telephone:
Fax:

Date:
No. :
Your Order No. :

Sold To:
   *
   *
   *

Shipped To:
   *
   *
   *

Our No.	Salesperson	Terms	F.O.B.	Ship Date	Shipped Via

Ordered	Shipped	Description	Unit Price	Amount

–THANK YOU FOR YOUR ORDER–
(prices subject to change without notice)

FREIGHT	
TOTAL DUE	$

Sample Broker Statement

Your Company Name
Broker Commission Statement

Broker Name: _____   Period From: _____   To: _____

	Date	Order	Account	Invoice Amount	Rate	Amount
1						
2						
3						
4						
5						
6						
7						
8						
9						
10						

TOTAL >>> _____

Comments: _____
_____
_____
_____

Total Commission: _____
Less Advance/Credit: _____
Commission Payable: _____

Sample Statement

STATEMENT

To:

| Number: |
| Statement Date: |
| Terms: |
| Customer No.: |

Item	Date	Description	Charge	Credit	Balance
		Previous Balance Brought Forward		>>>	

| Thank You For Your Business | | Please pay this amount | >>> | | |

Sample Dunning Letter (at the 33rd day)

Your Company Name
Address
Telephone Number

Date:
To:
Reference: Invoice number _____ of _____ (date)
Subject: Friendly reminder

To whom it may concern:

Our records indicate that the above referenced invoice remains unpaid.
Please comply with our terms and remit $ _____ to us immediately.

Let us know if your records do not concur with ours, and thank you for
your attention.

Sincerely,

Sample Dunning Letter (at the 45th day)

Your Company Name
Address
Telephone Number

Date:
To:
Reference: Invoice number _____ of _____ (date)
Subject: Second notice

To whom it may concern:

We still show an amount due of $ _____ for the referenced invoice.
Please contact us immediately if you feel there has been an error.
Otherwise we expect your remittance now.

Sincerely,

Sample Dunning Letter (at the 60th day)

Your Company Name
Address
Telephone Number

Date:
To:
Reference: Invoice number _____ of _____ (date)
Subject: Final Notice

To whom it may concern:

We have yet to receive payment of the referenced invoice. Since the amount due is now 60 days late, and in violation of our terms, we have no other recourse except to place your account into collection which we would rather not do. To avoid this unpleasant action, please remit $_____ now!

Sincerely,

Specialty Food Market Profile

A s part of your market research, you will find it useful to know something about current product category trends in the specialty food industry. More comprehensive information is contained in a study available from Packaged Facts, 581 Avenue of the Americas, New York, NY 10011, 212-627-3228, Web site: <www.marketresearch.com>. This is a 426-page report for $1,750, published in March 1998.

According to *New Product News*, there were 3,050 specialty/gourmet food products introduced to the market in 1999. The biggest category was Sauces, Seasonings, Condiments, Oils, and Vinegars (836), followed by Beverages (512).

The following is a brief profile of some of the major product categories, which includes discussion of product type, positioning, and circumstances that have impacted recent consumption trends.

Beverages

Specialty beverages include coffee and tea, bottled sparkling water, natural sodas, flavored seltzer, certain soft drinks, and juices.

The specialty beverage leaders are coffee and tea. In fact, coffee is the number one specialty product category. Major brand name coffee consumption has decreased over the past decade, but consumption of specialty coffees has increased. Much of the demand is for coffee beans that can provide a fresher cup than vacuumed-packed ground coffee. Decaffeinated coffee is in demand as well, along with flavored coffees.

Most specialty coffees are promoted on the strength of their freshness and taste. Many are offered as special blends, among which Irish Cream, Chocolate, Amaretto, and Hazelnut are best sellers.

Specialty tea is especially strong as a category, and includes both tea products and a variety of other non-camellia sinensis (tea) forms, including tonics, infusions, barks, and the like. As with coffee, overall consumption of tea is down, but consumption of specialty teas is up.

Specialty tea is sold in both loose and tea bag varieties. It is positioned in all kinds of retail outlets, and has shown a marked sales increase in fancy restaurants and hotels.

An example of a successful specialty tea transitioning from the specialty market to exclusively supermarket is Celestial Seasonings. This product can no longer be considered a specialty food product. Another tea line, Twinings, appears to successfully straddle the line between grocery and specialty distribution, depending on the varietal blend. For example, Twining's English Breakfast and Earl Grey teas are most likely to be seen in supermarkets, while its Lapsang Souchong and Russian Caravan varieties remain solidly placed in the specialty market.

The market for bottled sparkling water has many variants in the specialty food industry. Most major brands are now distributed outside of specialty food channels. These brands include San Peligreno, Poland Spring, Perrier, Evian, Adirondack, Ty Nant, etc.

Who knew that we would become so concerned with our tap water that we would spend billions of dollars on bottled versions that, by regulation, have to meet standards no more rigorous than those for tap water?

Sodas, seltzer, soft drinks, non-alcoholic spritzers, and certain juices comprise the remainder of this category.

Cheese and Dairy Products

In the 1980s, the specialty cheese sector was one of the fastest growing in the gourmet food market. In the 1990s, increased consumer awareness of so-called "healthy" foods influenced a decline in sales of the high-fat varieties. Brie remains in strongest demand, followed by aged cheddar, fresh curd cheese, soft ripened cheese, Swiss cheese, and blue mold cheese.

Goat's milk and sheep's milk cheeses have surged in popularity during the past five years. Both goat's and sheep's milk cheese are available in fresh versions (goat "Montrachet"), ripened versions (French "Boucheron"), and hard versions (French sheep's Pyrenees cheeses and Spanish sheep's milk hard cheeses).

Some specialty food stores carry several dozen cheese varieties; hence, with this kind of variety, most consumers have yet to develop a brand preference.

To further busy this market, producers have introduced light-style cheese and even newer varieties, such as chevre (goat) cheese. European-style cheese has been introduced by U.S. producers, and by U.S. manufacturing subsidiaries of overseas cheese companies. It is in this latter area that the greatest opportunity for specialty cheese growth exists.

Another specialty food product in this category is super-premium ice cream and frozen yogurt. The former came charging into the market in the 1970s, led by Häagen Dazs. By our definition, this can no longer be considered a specialty food. Despite the huge fat content, super-premium ice cream is an example of an affordable luxury—some go so far as to tout its medicinal value (eases emotional stress, etc.)—and there are numerous regional super-premium ice creams on the market. Notable is the Ben & Jerry's brand. Many are hand-packed and offer the consumer exotic flavors such as Praline Caramel Swirl and Mint Chocolate.

Watch for this category to be picked up increasingly by the major ice cream producers as they attempt to clone the flavor and fat content offered by the smaller producers.

The other notable part of this category is frozen yogurt, especially soft-served. Growth in frozen yogurt consumption now exceeds that of super-premium ice cream, especially the low-fat and fat-free varieties. Even Häagen Dazs now offers a branded frozen yogurt. Still, most frozen yogurt is made and sold in the same place, making it an improbable product for you to consider selling in retail packages.

There being only so much room in the nation's freezer cases, it is unlikely that you will be able to garner a niche without a sizable investment. The frozen food segment, in total, is considered to be the hardest to penetrate in the food industry. This is no less the case with super premium ice cream and frozen yogurt.

Crackers and Breads

Crackers are more important to consumers than cookies, according to a U.S. Department of Commerce report. In its Annual Household Penetration of Selected Grocery Items, the Department noted that crackers held more than 98 percent versus 95 percent for cookies. Even so, cookies account for more than 50 percent of the total snack foods market.

In the specialty food industry, crackers are used to serve other products, such as cheese and dips. Yet, a cracker product in grocery stores tends to be positioned as a food product in and of itself with its own characteristic flavor.

The big sellers tend to be high in fiber and low in salt. They appeal to a broad consumer interest in health and fitness. An even newer product type is the fat-free or low-fat cracker. Nearly every specialty food store carries a variety of specialty crackers.

Your chance to make a dent will be based on your ability to produce a unique cracker. It appears that the major food companies have been eager to copy successful specialty crackers under their own brands. Examples have included Keebler's "Stone Creek," Nabisco's "American Classic" line, and Pepperidge Farm's (a Campbell Soup subsidiary) "Distinctive Crackers" line. The cracker segment is a big one, with a wide assortment, and consumers always seem interested in trying new varieties.

Breads, on the other hand, are positioned differently than crackers. Breads include the bake-off variety that are offered fresh by the retailer. This segment includes French and Italian breads, rolls, bagels, and other types. They also include crispbreads and Lavosh that are baked, packaged, and shipped in retail containers.

A related product is potato chips, especially those that are prepared with low sodium and fat content. Also growing in popularity are tortilla chips made from various types of corn.

Condiments

The specialty condiments' segment of the specialty market constitutes hundreds of products. Among them are mustard, sauce, catsup, relish, salsa, pepper, olives, horseradish, mayonnaise, vinegar, herbs and spices, and seasoning.

Most are positioned as high quality, exotic, uniquely-flavored products compared to the grocery trade variants. The specialty condiment category has produced many of the products that have become mainstream grocery products. An example is Grey Poupon Dijon mustard. Distribution of this white wine-flavored variant began in the specialty food industry. It is now available in every supermarket and in almost all restaurants.

The dominant condiment is mustard. With more than five dozen brands on the market at any time, each manufacturer attempts to provide the ever-experimenting consumer with yet another taste sensation. Those that survive do so with a true sense of focused niche marketing, such as mustard with watercress, walnut, Roquefort, etc. Use of mustard has expanded from flavoring meats to creating dressings and use as sandwich spreads. These are accelerating use in the home, which means more mustard sales.

Other specialty condiments include chutney, extra virgin olive oils, flavored vinegars, avocado oils, spice pastes, flavored mayonnaise, salad dressings, and a variety of Tex-Mex, Caribbean, Thai, and stir-fry sauces. A recent entry is a green olive stuffed with a sun-dried tomato.

Specialty herbs, spices, and seasonings form an important and growing part of the specialty condiment segment. Many are offered as fresh-packaged herb blends, or as dips and mixes that can be blended easily with mayonnaise, yogurt, and/or sour cream to make a tasty and interesting hors d'oeuvre or appetizer.

Specialty condiments are positioned in a variety of packages, including glass jars, plastic, and aseptic containers, and tubes. Only shelf-stable salad dressings stick to the traditional long-necked salad dressing jar.

Specialty Meat and Seafood

Ranch buffalo, pâté de foie gras, country pâtés, terrines, unusual sausage, boar, venison, fowl, escargot, and certain deli meats are included in the specialty meat category. Seafood includes smoked salmon, caviar, eel, and certain fish.

Sales of these products are driven by consumers characterized by ethnic demographics. Their interest is in taking foods they remember from their experience in another country, or from association with particular ethnic habits and traditions.

Specialty fish consumption is on the increase, primarily due to consumer interest in its lower fat and cholesterol content. As a result, there has been an increase in aquaculture devoted to farming and marketing specialty fish, especially smoked salmon, smoked trout, and catfish.

Confection

The category includes chocolate, cakes, cookies, and candy. This is where the term "sinfully delicious" has the most meaning. Specialty confections appeal to a broad audience comprising people of all backgrounds and ages. Their allure is nearly universal—truly, the affordable luxury.

About this industry the saying goes, tongue in cheek: "What I need is another chocolate and another mustard line." Talk about widely over assorted! In any case, chocolate reigns with new varieties introduced every day. One is a 5" x 7" Chocolate Macadamia Monet painting, in which a painting by Claude Monet is brushed on a chocolate base with special confectioner's paint. Another example is a solid chocolate cellular phone!

Chocolate is now sold both in chocolate boutiques (Godiva, as an example), and in fancy retail packages. We pay upwards of $25 a pound for this indulgence. Very few chocolates have been successfully branded in the specialty food industry. Most that have succeeded did so with strong capital backing by large overseas chocolate companies, such as Tobler, Lindt, and Cadbury.

Many American chocolate companies have introduced high quality products. What distinguishes most of them from the rest is the inclusion of cocoa butter that provides high quality chocolate with a distinctive aroma and smoothness. This, plus interesting retail packaging and extensive promotion, helps carve out a profitable niche.

Specialty cookies are noted for their high quality content and imaginative ingredients. Among these are delicious tasting pistachio rum, double chocolate macadamia nut, and a variety of fancy chocolate chip cookies.

Other varieties include high quality, low-fat, and no-fat, cookies, and biscuits imported from Italy (panetonne), France, and Great Britain (shortbread).

Fancy cakes, those with extremely rich tasting ingredients (mostly chocolate), and with generous infusions of alcohol flavorings, have made a dent in the industry. Most are positioned for the hotel and restaurant trade, but many are sold via fancy retail outlets. They tend to be special occasion cakes, with strong seasonal sales. Many supermarkets have upgraded their baking products by offering made-to-order fancy cakes. Among the most popular appear to be carrot cake and fancy chocolate cake.

Specialty candies make up the remainder of the category and the best examples are imported hard candies from Europe and Japan. Most make their inroad by offering flavors not ordinarily associated with candy, such as kiwi and mango fruit. Others have caught consumer interest by being favored by famous people (personality endorsements), such as "gourmet" jelly beans. Even though few of these meet our definition of a specialty product, many have been introduced successfully through the specialty food trade.

Jams, Jellies, and Preserves

A vast assortment of jams, jellies, and preserves has been made available to the consumer by major food processors. An even wider assortment is available from cottage industries. It is from the latter that many of the new specialty food products have grown.

In both cases, the highest quality products are those that have little or no added sugar (some are sweetened only with apple or grape juice), no pectin, no artificial colors or flavors, and no preservatives. The imported jams and preserves with highest quality are those where the ingredients indicate more fruit than sugar.

Almost the entire market consists of retail packaged product. A small percentage is made available in bulk sizes for institutional and food service use, with some packaged in small containers for restaurant, airline service, and table top use.

Success, in terms of developing large volume, will be limited to the major producers, or, as in the case of Polaner All Fruit jams, to those producers who offer a new product at the right price not available from the major companies. It is much too easy to clone a jelly or jam recipe to suggest that yours will take over shelf space from Kraft or Welch's.

Keep in mind that Americans consume jam once a day, at breakfast, while Europeans slather jams onto afternoon tea biscuits, or make glazes using preserves, so usage in the United States is more limited than in Europe. This puts pressure on manufacturers who must pay for their space (slotting allowances), have their products sit among dozens of other options, and watch their product get consumed ever so slowly in this habitually breakfast-only scenario.

Food to Go

Prepared foods are offered by many, if not all, specialty food retail stores. They are of the type and quality one would expect from a consumer demanding both high quality ingredients and good taste.

This is among the fastest growing segment of the specialty food industry. It is especially popular with the DINKS (double income, no kids) population segment, because it offers quick and easy solutions to dinner preparation. The food is high quality fast food far removed from delivered pizza. One can purchase, all at once, a cold fruit soup, a freshly baked smoked-ham-and-brie tart, or an asparagus lasagna, and a rich, calorie-laden dessert. Most foods to go are sold from a refrigerated case, and very few are branded.

What you need to know about prepared specialty foods will help only if you are planning to open a retail outlet, or sell a locally prepared refrigerated product to retailers in your region. By the time you go beyond that area, the product falls into another category—a retail packaged food that will require some preparation before it can be consumed.

Miscellaneous Specialty Foods

This category involves the remainder of specialty food items. It includes, among others, pasta, mushrooms, rice, snack food, baked goods, soups, honey, truffles, vegetables, legumes, fruits, and rice.

One of the leaders is pasta, which follows understandably from the growing consumption of the category. Average annual consumption now exceeds 17 pounds per capita.

Mushroom consumption has increased also, especially for fresh mushrooms. More than three quarters of all mushrooms are sold fresh, just the opposite of what pertained 20 years ago when most mushrooms were sold processed. The specialty mushrooms, which include shitake, morel, Italian Brown, and chanterelle are sold in both fresh and processed versions. They appeal to a small audience, largely composed of chefs and institutional food service accounts. Kennett Square, for example, is bursting with business, selling their fresh mushrooms to consumers, not only chefs. Portobelo, a brown version of the classic white mushroom, has gained wide popularity simply because of its color.

Wild rice, especially Basmati and American wild, are available in dry packages and as rice mixes. Most of the growth for American rice is abroad. Italian Arborio and Carnaroli are used as the bases for Risotto, a quick to develop entree in Italian restaurants.

Snackfoods abound, and most in the specialty industry consist of high quality dried fruits, nuts, trail mixes, and certain crackers. Successful specialty snackfoods are those that have the right combination of high quality and low price in order to appeal to a wide audience.

Specialty soups are available in numerous varieties. Notable among them are the Knorr's, Mayacamma, Pepperidge Farm, and Baxters (from Scotland). Most of these tend not to duplicate available flavors. Royal Game, Pheasant, Lobster Bisque, Mulagatawny, Senegalese, and Vegetable Korma are some of the fancy soups now on the market.

The proliferation of dried soup mixes versus canned, condensed, or ready-to-serve soups is apparent. Producing these requires less capital, and shipping and storing the product is less expensive for the new specialty food marketer.

Produce has always played a part in the specialty food market. Fruits, such as the kiwi and mango, and vegetables, such as salad greens and the already mentioned mushrooms, continue to offer up interesting variations for the consumer. Your only interest in this category probably will be for personal consumption, unless you want to use an interesting vegetable or dried fruit in a specialty retail packaged concoction.

Much of the growth of miscellaneous specialty foods will come from expanding consumer interest generated from exposure to designer menus in upscale, health, and nutrition-oriented restaurants.

Summary

Success in the specialty food industry can be achieved by those entrepreneurs willing to adopt the specialty food perspective. Such a perspective requires a willingness to accept a floating bottom line, as well as strong perseverance, and a skilled promotional savvy.

Regardless of your approach, a knowledge of industry trends, competition, and stimulants and constraints to product growth will be invaluable to the new product marketer.

Current and Future Trends

Analyzing and predicting trends in any market is a multilayered task. Trends affecting the food industry as a whole can usually be seen in each specific market, such as the case of convenience and better-for-you foods in the specialty trade. Trends also have a tendency to feed and play off of one another as well, with each lasting a varied amount of time before either falling off the consumer's radar or becoming a staple.

Trends in the marketplace influence every consumer's behavior. Trends affect the food industry on a zillion levels from specific food choices to changing meal patterns.

Not all trends are the same. Some are pervasive, influencing the whole social landscape, others are really just fads. Trends have a life cycle, and the particular stage of a trend is critical in determining its connection to a particular product or service.

Trends can exist on many levels. For instance, we can talk about a growing penchant for hot foods or dining at home. If both are trends, might one explain the other? Does an understanding of one general sociological trend help explain a specific food trend?

How Do Trends Relate to Food Marketing?

Successful businesses are market driven when they design their products and services to fulfill consumer needs. They can define the marketplace through demographics (identifiable, measurable characteristics such as age, economic status, ethnic background, etc.), and psychographics (lifestyle or attitude characteristics).

Knowledge of today's trends can help you develop products and promotions for the future. The world is changing at an accelerated pace. Not much looks as it did 50 years ago. Like every other industry, the food industry has had to adapt to consumer demands driven by changing lifestyles.

What Is Happening with New Products in the Specialty Food Market Right Now?

The Convenience Bug Bites Specialty Foods

As we enter the 21st century fully embracing the information age, consumers have warmed to the spoils of convenience. It is no longer a luxury, but a way of life. The notion of convenience is a trend we have seen driving the food industry across the board. Specialty foods, as always, have their own special niche.

Convenient specialty foods are very different from the precooked or frozen quick menu items such as the all-ingredients in the bag Convenient Meal Solutions found in supermarkets. Specialty food consumers could be considered "foodies," as they are people who love food and more importantly, love to cook. They may be as short on time as the average consumer, but passively heating an entree in the microwave does not interest them.

Products such as premixed spices, marinades, and sauces, washed and cut produce, and even dry mixes for ethnic dishes, make it easy for even a two-income household to actively cook a meal in less time than ever before. Snacking is no different. Specialty food manufacturers are sympathizing with the busy consumer who needs a quick meal with upscale versions of Lunchables or similar cheese and cracker preparations. Prepackaged cheese and organic crackers, or pitas and hummus are becoming the discerning consumer's quick fix.

Gourmet and Natural Food Stores Blurring Their Lines

Another across the board trend is the emergence of "better-for-you" foods. The focus has shifted in the last decade from taking the bad

The substance of this appendix has been provided by the editorial staff of the Global New Products Database (GNPD), published by Mintel International Group Ltd. GNPD is the premier source of global new product introduction information. It is updated daily and provides extensive detail on new product introductions, including photography and ingredient statements. Mintel also provides product retrieval and quality assurance services. You may obtain more information on this downloadable, searchable database and other company services by calling 312-932-0400 or visiting their Web site at <www.gnpd.com>.

things out (fat, calories) to putting good ones in, or promoting the inherent goodness of some foods (added calcium, functional foods, organics). This being the case, one cannot refer to the specialty foods market without also considering the natural foods industry. The organic food and beverage category, for example, is growing at better than 20 percent per year.

The emergence of successful chains like Whole Foods and Wild Oats has caused today's consumer image of health foods to fade. Taking its place is the natural foods image, one of all-natural, premium ingredients, and if not organic, at least made with no preservatives or additives. That same description could also be used to describe many of today's specialty foods. The wide assortment of imported cheese, meats, and baked goods on display in any Whole Foods store would be just as comfortable in a specialty setting.

More than ever we are seeing specialty foods bearing kosher and organic certification. Labels boast of the contents being all-natural and containing no preservatives. The lines are blurring as many of the same brands find themselves in both markets. The result is an identity crisis because food products wind up appealing to the senses in both taste, look, smell, and health benefit.

Ethnic Flavors

Now more than ever the face of the nation is changing in terms of ethnic makeup. Hispanic and Oriental populations, not to mention others, are increasing at a steady rate. In turn, their cultures are influencing the way we eat.

Some time in the 1990s, "spaghetti" became "pasta," and ethnic foods, even Italian, experienced a renaissance as our interest increased. Specialty consumers are quick to embrace the new tastes and ways of cooking ethnic foods provide. Convenience items such as dry Indian Biryani Mixes to flavored tortillas, again make it easier than ever for consumers to dive into ethnic cooking.

Perhaps the most widespread embrace of an ethnic flavor in the past few years has been the emergence of Chai. The centuries-old formula of black tea leaves mixed with milk, sweetener, cinnamon, and other spices is most prominently seen in coffee and tea drinks but is also now showing up in products like specialty ice cream.

Imported Products

Another area affected by the changing face of our population is the emergence of imported products. Certain foods may be commonplace in their country of origin, but considered a specialty item here. Often this is the case simply because we don't have the resources to produce the products ourselves. They become specialty items because of the price point demanded to get the products on the shelves. Also, the mainstream consumer's taste preferences may not be as accepting as those of the specialty food consumer.

Due to the increasing popularity of ethnic foods, products such as extra virgin olive oils, olives, cheese, and seasonings from all over the world are experiencing increased popularity in specialty markets.

Hand-Crafted Products

An important quality that sets specialty foods apart from the rest is the special care and quality put into the manufacturing of the product. The story of starting the line in your own kitchen in handmade batches is a familiar one to the industry.

Consumers look for and expect the hand-crafted quality that specialty foods provide. Again, the "foodie" element comes into play. To them, the appearance and pedigree of a product, from confections and chocolates to condiments, are just as important as the taste.

Retailers, too, seem to look to this trend to help them sell specialty foods. Many stores have sections containing locally-made products, and a tour of any specialty food store will reveal a number of faces on product packages—clearly bringing home the concept that someone is in the kitchen cooking up food just for you.

Premium Priced Products and More Expensive Ingredients and Packaging

In turn, hand-crafted products lead to premium priced items. A specialty food consumer is not one to flinch at the higher prices specialty foods command. In fact, an association between the price and quality of the product is often made: "The more it costs the better it must be."

It is also the nature of specialty foods to demand a higher price point due to imported items, hard-to-find ingredients used, or limited quantities being available. In addition, many of these products sport creative, unusual, keepsake packaging. The high-quality ingredients and upscale packaging are two major factors that set specialty foods apart from mainstream fare.

Another point of interest concerning premium prices is that sales of many premium priced foods do not significantly decline during modest economic downturns. Why? Consumers treat themselves to small indulgences (such as a gourmet jar of pickles for $10) rather than some of the bigger indulgences they may have enjoyed in fatter times. Specialty foods have long been considered an affordable luxury.

What's Around the Corner?
Predictions for the Specialty Food Market

Fusion Confusion

With the rise of "nutraceuticals" and "functional foods," plus the growing number of ingredients that offer specific health benefits, more and more food products will make medical claims. On the flip side, more medicinal products will come in food-type forms that taste good.

Awareness is growing among American consumers regarding the concept of genetically-modified organisms (GMOs). Watch for more GMO-free products to hit the shelves.

Oh Boy . . . It's Soy

Thanks to government research showing soy's cardiac/cancer benefits, manufacturers will introduce a host of soy ingredient products. Research has shown that soy is also good for the skin and helps curb many health problems suffered by women such as osteoporosis and the development of breast cancer, so look for it in face and body care products as well.

Pick on Someone Your Own Size

As mainstream stores become more crowded and the cost of entry becomes prohibitive, major players in the supermarket industry will seek out smaller markets, guerrilla style. That is, major companies will target gourmet stores with specialty food divisions that, on the surface, bear no resemblance and have no apparent affiliation with any large company. A case in point is Kellogg's Country Inn Specialties cereal line.

Designer Diner

Consumers will take a cue from restaurants to whip up their own modernized "designer diner" versions of classic favorites. Making it all possible will be simplified cooking time in the kitchen thanks to the increasing number of high quality "speed scratch" items now available.

Cuisine of the Future

Consumer interest in all forms of ethnic cuisine, in particular, Latino and Asian dishes, is continuing to increase. Look for more popularity among these two groups, with emphasis placed on specific, regional fare. As the world shrinks thanks to satellite TV and the Internet, we will be more aware of, and more apt to explore, regional dishes rather than the generic terms of Italian or Mexican.

Year-Round Gifts

Why are foods as gifts only popular at Christmas? People give and receive gifts year round and fancy foods are always welcome. Food gifts are available online, but not so easy to find in supermarkets. Watch for large supers to set up in-store food gift departments (in the flower shop?) to keep "em comin in."

Rummage Sale

Manufacturers often find themselves wanting to relieve modest sales performers, not necessarily do away with them. Specialty entrepreneurs will take a cue from companies like Aurora Foods, that has taken to marketing "orphan" food brands neglected by others.

Easy as 1, 2, 3

More and more manufacturers are playing the Numbers Game. Six-cheese variety blends, 20-grain cereals, 12-grain breads, eight-fruit juices, four-grain pancake mixes. Assuming more is better, expect an increase in multi-ingredient foods.

How to Interpret These Trends

Understanding the implications of these trends will improve your ability to predict markets. The first step is to understand that a trend—a general tendency of events—is driven by forces that change over time. Consider, also, that no one trend operates in a vacuum. All trends interact, sometimes reinforcing each other, other times canceling each other out.

The challenge is to relate underlying forces to the trends pervading our social climate and more specifically to specific food trends. When we do that, we have a much better chance of making accurate predictions. For instance, if spicy foods are "hot," does that mean we are seeing a long-lasting trend? We have more clues when we understand that spicy food usually infers an ethnic orientation. It also is part of the blending and blurring in our society. Home Meal Replacement simply makes it easier to consume ethnic food. So, indeed, we could argue that this trend could be around for a while.

Specialty Food Trends Resource List

How to Find Out about Underlying Forces and Changing Trends

Good sources of trend information appear in the media. This includes the Internet, which is being used with increasing frequency as a communication means. Several resources look at what's going on in the marketplace. Targeted to varying audiences, they each have their own focus and format. What they have to say is extremely valuable for developing staying power in the food world. Make your job easier by learning what the experts are saying. In addition to the professional trade journals listed in Appendix A, the following may be useful in developing a deeper understanding of consumer trends and their impact on specialty food marketing.

Publications

ACNielsen
177 Broad Street, Stamford, CT 06901.
203-961-3000
Web site: <www.anielsen.com>

Provides sales data and analysis of mainly supermarket product activity.

American Demographics, Magazine of Consumer Trends
PO Box 68
Ithaca, NY 14851
800-350-3060

"Check-Out Line" focuses on items sold in supermarkets. Subscriptions are $69 annually.

The Food Channel Newsletter
Editor: Chris Wolf, e-mail: chris.wolf@noble.net
Strategic Foods Resources
Division of Noble Associates
Springfield, MO and Chicago, IL
417-875-5129; Fax: 417-875-5051

An electronic newsletter that includes *Food Trend News, HotBytes*, and *Late-Breaking*. The newsletter is distributed four times monthly to subscribers, clients, and media. Individual e-letter subscriptions are $195 per year. Corporate subscriptions are $895. For subscription inquiries, contact Debbie Merritt.

Foodwatch
Eleanor Hanson, Editor/Publisher
125 Thatcher Avenue
River Forest, IL, 60305-2020
708-366-4599

Reporting consumer food trends, tracking, analysis, and insights drawn from their review of newspapers from ten major U.S. cities and 20 popular consumer magazines. Published monthly in alternating formats: a 10-page publication and a one-page "QuickBites," billed as culinary grazing. Subscriptions are $48 per year.

New Product News
New Product News (NPN) Subscription Services
Attn.: Mr. Branton Maratoya
213 West Institute Place, Suite 208
Chicago, IL 60610
312-932-0400; Fax: 312-932-0469

NPN does not have a Web site. Annual subscription is $795; single issues $80.

The Global New Products Database
Lynn Dornblaser, Editorial Director
213 W. Institute Place, Suite 208
Chicago, IL 60610
312-932-0600

Incorporates trade publication *New Product News*, and provides information and analysis on new product introductions and trends.

SPINS Research
185 Berry St.
San Francisco, CA 94107
415-284-0546
Web site: <www.spencinfo.com>

SPINS collects sales data from mainly natural food stores, unlike IRI or Nielsen.

Trend/wire Newsletter
P.O. Box 6217
Leawood, KS 66206
913-648-7492

Essential for those seeking to break into the foodservice market. Editor/guru Art Siemering offers information, analysis, and humor with each issue. Subscriptions are $175 per year.

The Popcorn Report
by Faith Popcorn
Institute of Food Technology
221 N. LaSalle Street
Chicago, IL 60601
312-782-8424

Published by HarperBusiness, 1991 Food Institute Report, August, 1994.

Miscellaneous Resources

The following listing is neither conclusive nor is it meant to serve as an endorsement.

Business Lists

Info USA, Inc.
5711 S. 86th Circle
Omaha, NE 68127
402-331-7169
Web site: <www.infousa.com>

Business listings compiled from nationwide Yellow Pages.

Gourmet News
POB 1056
Yarmouth, ME 04096
207-846-0800

Rents its extensive listing of specialty food decision-makers.

Nutritional Analysis and Labeling

Strasburger & Seigel, Inc.
1229 National Drive
Hanover, MD 21076

800-875-6532 or 410-712-7373
Fax: 410-712-7378
Web site: <www.sas-labs.com>

Strasburger and Siegel is just one of many laboratories that offer competitively-priced analytical services including microbiological and microanalytical services, consulting services (project design, product stability and shelf-life evaluation, thermal process engineering, etc.), and customized product development services.

See also Lawerence-Allen Group NutriLABEL on page 198 of Appendix K.

NutriPower
400 Washington Street, #LL6
Braintree, MA 02184
617-356-8700

A computer program that creates all Nutrition Facts formats.

Produce Marketing

Sell What You Sow! The Grower's Guide to Successful Produce Marketing
New World Publishing
3085 Sheridan Street
Placerville, CA 95667
916-622-2248

Sell What You Sow! by Eric Gibson, is a guide to profitable produce marketing that covers marketing plans, research, crop selection, and selling through farmer's markets, restaurants, roadside markets, pick-your-own operations, and retail outlets. It is a comprehensive how-to book of high-value produce marketing.

Quality Issues

A couple of good sources for improving your knowledge of quality and productivity are:

The Deming Route to Quality and Productivity
William W. Scherkenbach
CEEPress Books
George Washington University, 1992

The Memory Jogger
Michael Brassard and Diane Ritter
GOAL/QPC, 1994
800-643-4316

This is a pocket guide of tools for continuous improvement and effective planning.

Uniform Product Code

Uniform Code Council, Inc.
8163 Old Yankee Rd., Suite J
Dayton, OH 45458
513-435-3870

Contact: Harold P. Juckett, Executive Vice President
The Uniform Code Council is the central management and information center for manufacturers and retailers participating in the system. Current cost of registration is $300.

Women in the Food Industry
Office of Women's Business Ownership
U.S. Small Business Administration
1110 Vermont Street NW
Washington, DC 20416
202-606-4000, 800-827-5722

Roundtable for Women in Foodservice Inc.
425 Central Park West, Suite 2A
New York, NY 10025
800-898-2849; Fax: 212-688-6457

Count Me In for Women's Economic Independence (Women and Money)
Web site: <www.count-me-in.org>
e-mail: info@count-me-in.org

Count Me In for Women's Economic Independence is a national nonprofit organization that will raise money from women—to be loaned to women. Count Me In is a lending and learning organization dedicated to strengthening women's position in the economy. The concept is straightforward: millions of women across America will be asked—and inspired—to contribute a minimum of $5 to Count Me In to create a national loan fund for women. The money will be redistributed to qualifying women in the form of small business loans ranging from $500 to $10,000 and scholarships for business training and technical assistance.

Index